HIDDEN
HISTORY
of
WALT DISNEY
WORLD

Foxx Nolte

THE
History
PRESS

Published by The History Press
Charleston, SC
www.historypress.com

Cover photo courtesy of Orlando Public Library.
Opposite: 1972 Map of Florida. *Author's collection.*

First published 2024

Manufactured in the United States

ISBN 9781467156189

Library of Congress Control Number: 2023947099

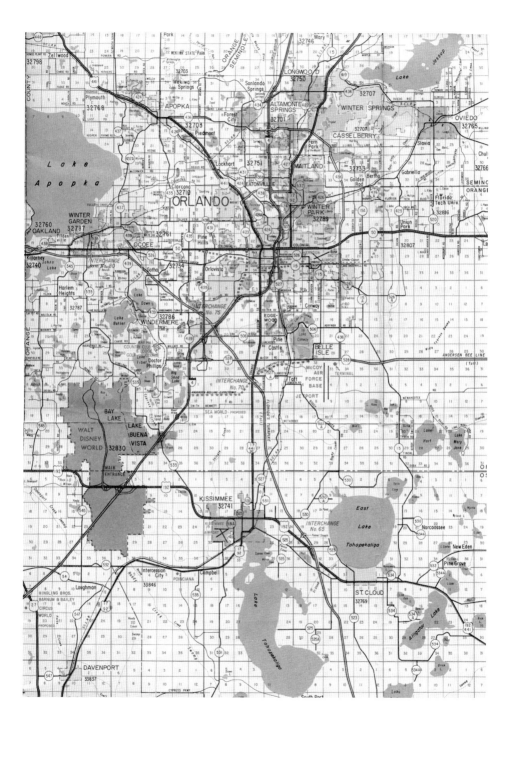

CONTENTS

PREFACE

Chambers of Commerce in Florida for fifty years have had paid executives who have gone out and said to people up north: "Come on down!"…I'm telling you they all got here at one time.
—*Orlando mayor Carl Langford, 1972*

Walt Disney World's history is vast, baffling and complex—pretty much like the place itself. This book is tiny. It would be impossible to adequately cover the entire history of Walt Disney World in a book of this size, so I'm not even going to try. Instead, my aim is to introduce history into your vacation by connecting it to places you can actually go to, with an emphasis on the strange and surprising.

By focusing on these smaller pieces of the history, this book piece by piece builds a larger narrative about how Walt Disney World was created and how it became what it is today. By necessity, it focuses pretty much exclusively on the resort's tumultuous first quarter century, when it was shaped.

I hope I have left enough of a breadcrumb trail to entice readers to find out more about this fascinating place themselves. In the end, this isn't the most all-encompassing overview of the "Florida Project," but I do hope it'll be the most surprising and fun.

O.98   AIRPLANE VIEW OF BUSINESS SECTION, SHOWING PART OF LAKE EOLA

ORLANDO, FLA., "THE CITY BEAUTIFUL"   N-M-D AIR PHOTO, ORLANDO

Vintage postcard showing Downtown Orlando in the 1930s. *Author's collection.*

Prelude

THE FATAL GLASS OF BEER

It was 1963, and Walt Disney was in Missouri.

Specifically, he was appearing before the city council of St. Louis to pitch his idea for a "Midwest Disneyland." Walt Disney's Riverfront Square was to be a massive building the size of three city blocks containing an indoor re-creation of gaslight St. Louis. Inside were to be versions of attractions currently being developed for Disneyland, including the "Blue Bayou Adventure" and a "Haunted House." St. Louis residents were excited, and plans were proceeding quickly.

Joe Fowler—Walt's can-do construction guy—told the story years later:

> *Riverfront Square was only two blocks from Anheuser Busch Stadium. And of course August Busch was a great man in St. Louis....We had a big banquet the night before the final papers were to be signed. Walt was there. The Mayor of St. Louis was sitting beside me. Then Mr. Busch got up and he said, "Any man that thinks he can open and make a success of any amusement park and not sell beer or hard liquor ought to have his head examined." Walt was sitting beside me, and I saw that eyebrow go up!*

Had this banquet been put on by Disney Studio employees instead of St. Louis politicians, that eyebrow raising would have chilled the blood of everyone in the room. Disney employees knew what that look meant. Soon, Riverfront Square was abandoned, and planning for Walt Disney World was underway.

I hope you enjoyed that story. It's tidy and dramatic.

I intended on telling that story as the opening chapter of this book—except when I went to verify it, it turned out it wasn't true at all.[1] Well, sort of. It wasn't entirely false either. Like a lot of stories about Walt Disney, it's a true-ish version of a complicated situation.

These stories exist because Walt Disney told them. As author Beth Dunlop put it, Walt Disney was a "master at conjuring fictional memories."[2]

For just a representative smattering from his life story, consider Walt inventing Mickey Mouse on the train ride home after losing his animation studio or dreaming up Disneyland while watching his children ride a carousel. Walt Disney always wanted to present the simplest and best version of any story. As Walt always told his animation staff: "No contradictions—no ambiguities." In this case, we can see that Joe Fowler was honoring Walt's memory by telling a Walt Disney–style story. The company has kept telling those stories over the course of its one-hundred-year history; if you picked up this book, you probably have been exposed to a few of them.

So, while you and I are standing out here in this vast Florida wilderness stepping on fantasies, I suppose we should begin by squashing the big one.

Walt Disney, the man who gave his name to the most famous vacation destination in the world, had almost nothing to do with Walt Disney World. Yes, he set the plan in motion; yes, he gave the order to buy the land. Yes, there are statues and tributes and weird souvenir coffee mugs with his image on them. But Walt Disney was dead and gone by the time any real planning took place, any land was moved or any paying customer set foot on red concrete.

But you know, that really gets to the core of what makes Walt Disney World so fascinating, so good. Walt Disney doing something amazing is a day ending in -y, but his creative heirs doing it? Bringing to life this amazing place based entirely on the legacy of a dead man? That's a real story. And that is the story of this book.

Walt Disney may not be a major player in it, but the history of Walt Disney World is a history of backroom politics, urban planning, wild ambitions and failed schemes. It traces the story of a giant mass of virgin land that by turns almost became an oil field, a city of the future, an institutional research center, a movie studio backlot and even a tennis ball factory. It's messy and weird and wonderful and not at all like the tidy stories Disney and its subsidiaries like to tell about themselves.

Most importantly, I hope that even if you merely sample these chapters, they will give you a fuller enjoyment of Walt Disney World, one above and

Walt Disney, William "Joe" Potter and Roy O. Disney. Two of these men would go on to open Walt Disney World. *Florida State Archives.*

beyond the "Disney version." That place may be all neat lawns and trim architecture and smiling faces, but below it has a real undercurrent of the bizarre so rich you can almost grab hold of it. Because the more you scratch at the surface of Walt Disney World, the weirder it gets.

PART I

• ——————————— •

MILES OF WORTHLESS LAND

I remember going down to Florida with Walt. We stood out in the middle of Interstate 4, right on the highway. I looked both ways, and there wasn't a car in sight, and I said, "Walt, are you sure this is the place you want to put this thing?" And he said, "Don't you worry about it. They'll come from all directions, and we're putting it right here because it's in the middle."

—Wathel Rogers

1

In the Beginning,
There Was Bay Lake

I magine that you are standing on the shores of Bay Lake some hot Florida afternoon around 1994. The scene would look very much as it does now—the white-hot sunlight, the swaying Florida scrub pine, the sputter of those little canopied boats out on the water. Strolling the shore, you come across an old Florida pine and suddenly notice that there is something strange about this tree. On closer inspection, it's clear that an old push-style mower is embedded deep within the root system. Disney has posted a sign nearby:

> *Too long did Billy Bowlegs*
> *Park his reel slow mower*
> *Alas, one warm and sunny day*
> *Aside a real fast grower*

This detail, all too easy to pass by unnoticed, gnaws at your brain. It raises too many questions. The lawnmower and the tree are obviously much older than Walt Disney World, which raises a question: What was here before Disney?

When Disney bought its property in the 1960s, there were, as *Orlando Sentinel* columnist Charlie Wadsworth put it, "more deer than people."[3] But there were some people. Orlando is a city that lives on its lakes; in the old times, the street names—Ivanhoe, Apopka, Sand, Underhill, Turkey—simply indicated which lake they terminated at. Even in those quiet pre-

Bay Lake in its untouched state, circa 1963. *Florida State Archives.*

Disney days, Bay Lake was a remarkable natural phenomenon, and in Orlando, where there are lakes there are people. And so, in the beginning, truly at the heart of Walt Disney World, is Bay Lake.

Walt Disney may not have ever seen Walt Disney World, but he definitely saw Bay Lake. While flying over in the company jet, Disney looked out the window, saw Bay Lake and remarked, "There's Tom Sawyer Island—buy it!"[4]

Walt may have been only the latest millionaire to say those words, but so far, he's been the last. Before America had Hollywood studios or giant tech companies, it had railroads. A railroad company was the original owner of Bay Lake.

If we open the history books, we discover that Bay Lake and its signature island were owned by the Plant Railroad Company. Henry Plant's company divested itself of the island in 1887, and the property went through multiple owners before landing in the possession of one Joel Riles. The name Riles Island (sometimes incorrectly distorted to "Raz Island") has marked the island ever since. OK, get out your notepaper, this gets confusing fast.

Joel Riles neglected to pay taxes on his new island, and the property was reclaimed by the State of Florida. But Riles slipped everyone a Mickey

Radio Nick. *Courtesy of Orange County Regional History Center.*

and sold the island to a man named Jim Geer—presumably laughing himself silly on the way to the bank. Since the state had already gone and sold the defaulted property to the Reams family, this was a real problem, and Geer ended up buying out Reams.

Jim Geer may have regretted the choice, because this set off a chain of property disputes within his family that lasted for twenty years. Susan Geer, Jim's widow, finally sold the island to one Delmar Nicholson, who has gone down in Orlando legend as Radio Nick.

Radio Nick is one of those Orlando personalities where the more you research him, the more you can hardly believe that he was real. Radio Nick went to Philadelphia to study the new and exciting technological world of radio transmission. He returned to Orlando as a prince of the realm and opened his own high-class radio store—Radio Nick Inc.—at 23 Wall Street. And then things got weird.

Delmar's father was a reptile collector, and Radio Nick hosted multiple "snake shows" in town, which resulted in the hoi polloi of Orlando scurrying up onto the seats of their chairs as the reptiles broke loose into the room.

Nicholson advocated for the founding of a zoo in Orlando's Eola Park and collected many native animals for the purpose, installing them in a parcel three hundred feet square. Alligators and monkeys kept escaping, sending local residents into fits.

How's this for a look into the social life of Orlando in the mid-1930s? Let's check the *Orlando Star-Sentinel* on November 1, 1936, to see how Orlandoans spent their Halloween. Front-page article: "Eyeless Drive Secret Kept by Boardman":

> *The mystery of how Dr. Frank Boardman drove his Buick up and down Orange Avenue thru noon-day traffic yesterday with a black blindfold of four thicknesses over his eyes remained a mystery late last night. Most of Central Florida stood on the curb all the way up the avenue and saw Doc's classy looking sports job tear along at a 45-mile-an-hour clip, stop at all red lights, and never come close to having an accident. Doc claims that it is "par-optic" vision that enables him to do the trick. He says he has developed this "sightless" eye over a period of ten years and never revealed the secret.*[5]

Never one to let a show go unstolen, Delmar Nicholson arrived at the scene in an open-top car loaded with radio equipment and pretended to "guide" Boardman electronically as he made the drive. Onlookers bought it. The two of them must have howled in laughter at the bar that night.

On Christmas Eve, Nick liked to parade up and down Orange Avenue with an enormous porcelain duck (!) filled with whiskey, pouring out shots to any and all. When he ran out of whiskey, he refilled the duck at a saloon called the Brass Rail.[6] I promise you I'm not making this up.

Radio Nick bought Riles Island from Susan Geer in 1937, renamed the property Idle Bay Isle and began to plant tropical fruits there.[7] By 1941, the *Orlando Sentinel* could describe "the huge magnolia trees of Idle Bay Isle in full bloom." In 1944, he was hosting open houses on the island, showing off his lime, mango, papaya and avocado groves, all novelties in Central Florida. Nick's open houses were legendary and exclusive, featuring limeade made with his own crop. (Visitors were advised to bring their own sugar.)

Visitors were advised to drive the "Vineland Road," turn right at the sign that said "IBI" and proceed past Windermere to the shores of Bay Lake.[8] The *Sentinel* continued:

> *To reach the premises Nick has installed a siren at the shore landing which visitors sound to attract his attention. Nick then looks over his visitors from the island with powerful binoculars and if they are not "persona grata" he doesn't stir. For his friends, however, he starts up the put-put and goes after them.*[9]

Sadly, Radio Nick's fruit-based escapades came to an end in the mid-1950s, when the island again went through a series of sales, landing in the possession of a group of locals known as the Isle Bay Club that operated it as a fishing retreat. A fishing camp was built on the south shore of Bay Lake where the boat dock of Fort Wilderness is today. It's during this period that we have our fateful day when somebody left an old-fashioned lawnmower leaning on the side of a tree near Bay Lake.

And that is the way it remained until Disney bought the property in 1964. At that time, the fishing camp was derelict, given over to native wildlife and rambunctious locals. The latter is just a guess, for in 1971 local chronicler Charlie Wadsworth commented:

> *At about 10 pm the start of a brilliant fireworks display for which the name Disney is famous began. Naturally, the guests were delighted. And*

Radio Nick (*seated on left*) "Doc" Boardman (*blindfolded, center*) and an unidentified assistant mystifying onlookers. *Courtesy of the Orlando Public Library.*

Roy Disney tromps past the old fish camp on the shores of Bay Lake. *Florida State Archives.*

naturally, the residents of nearby Windermere were startled. There hadn't been a noise like that since some of the young bucks of the community used to get together on old Riles Island on Bay Lake. Only in those days they called that kind of activity "howling at the moon." [10]

In some ways, those years are back. In 1973, Disney leveled Nick's fruit groves, regraded the island and built a bird sanctuary called Treasure Island (in later days Discovery Island). The island closed to official visitors in 1998 and has since become famous as a location for illicit gallivanting about. For a close view, take one of the boat launches across Bay Lake and peer into the thick jungle of the only Disney theme "park" to have ever gone over into rack and ruin, a contrast to the orderly resort all around it.

One would think that the company would treat the island that motivated Walt Disney to open his wallet with a little more dignity.

But I like to imagine that on quiet Florida nights, the sound of '40s big-band music echoes across the water and the smell of unsweetened limeade can be detected on the breeze. It's the island that everybody wants to buy but only Radio Nick made his own.

The Oldest House
at Walt Disney World

OK, I can hear you saying, that may be well and good, but an eccentric radio mogul and snake wrangler using Riles Island to grow limes is not exactly what I had in mind. Well…really I'm not certain how anybody could dislike that answer, but I agree with you that that is not exactly habitation. Did anybody live at Disney World before it was Disney World?

Well, yes, there is one more example.

Today, motorists driving southbound from West Orlando and Windermere are likely to take Apopka-Vineland Road, a north–south artery that connects Lake Apopka to—well, we'll get to Vineland later. What's more important to know is simply that this road has existed since the 1930s and offered some of the few ways to get into the heart of what is now Disney property. This area was so remote that most maps of Central Florida from before the '60s don't even bother to detail it.

But out here is where Carl D. Bronson and a scant few others lived out a sweaty life. Bronson was a decorated U.S. Air Force pilot and lived on acres of virgin land to the east of what was then known as Black Lake. Orlando senator Bob Elrod later described this area as "the sorriest piece of land around.…You couldn't raise citrus on it. It wasn't even good for hunting."[11]

Carl Bronson's little three-room house, built sometime between 1957 and 1964, is the oldest structure at Walt Disney World. How that happened is as remarkable a story as anything else connected to the history of Disney. When Bronson sold out to the mysterious Reedy Creek Ranch on or about December 27, 1964, for the lordly sum of $93,400, the Walt Disney Company acquired his house, landing strip, airplane hangar, a grove and an unspecified amount of property surrounding. It was to sit empty for a year and a half.

In 1966, Phil Smith, Disney's Orlando lawyer, was offered the house as a rent-free option by the company, and so Phil and his family moved way out to where the cicadas sing with their two children. It was a remote lifestyle. "It felt a little strange out there. So absolutely quiet at night. And just as dark as sin," Smith recalled later.[12]

Disney had announced the occupancy of the Smith family in the *Orlando Sentinel*, so Phil was often pestered by job seekers. As a result, the family had a special relationship with the local law officer, who would hurry out to the property to hustle away any unwanted company. In return, Smith allowed the constable to hunt on the south side of Disney property and was often supplied with fresh venison.[13] Sometimes, Florida Traffic Control would make use of the Bronson airstrip.[14]

Smith and his family would often boat out to Riles Island, which they called Buzzard Island, probably making use of the same dock used by Radio Nick back in the '40s. By that time, the area east of Bay Lake was already beginning to be leveled, graded and transformed into Walt Disney World.

Dramatic changes were occurring all around their little house. By 1969, Disney had built a highway into Disney property to the Preview Center, which sat just across Black Lake. Moving out in 1968, the Smith family removed a few bricks from the fireplace of their little home as mementos of a remarkable time in their lives.

The little ranch home was not the only thing out on Carl Bronson's land in Vineland—he also had an airplane hangar and landing strip. What first seems to be mere eccentricity actually has a story behind it, as we learn in the *Orlando Sentinel* that Bronson operated a flight school in 1963 and 1964. He called the thing Air-Lando—not to be confused with rival flight school Air Orlando—and promised free "hot coffee, donuts, and Southern hospitality." The venture seems to have fizzled out within a few years, but it's intriguing to know that there was an attraction on Disney property before Disney!

The Bronson/Smith ranch home, July 2023. *Photo by the author.*

Today, the site of the Bronson/Smith house is approximately building 5501–836 of "The Paddock" section of Saratoga Springs Resort & Spa. The house itself was picked up and moved sometime in 1971 to a nonpublic area of property, where it has been renovated and exists today as an environmental lab.

Walt Disney World is home to a profusion of remarkable and apparently historic structures, from Victorian train stations to Hollywood movie palaces, but the most historic structure on property is hidden away on a narrow road out of sight.

TIME WARP ON BLACK LAKE

O n the other hand, history trippers can visit one location that is nearly as old and twice as interesting: the first public attraction to open at Walt Disney World. For sitting untouched and seemingly forgotten along the bustle of Hotel Plaza Boulevard near Disney Springs is the Walt Disney World Preview Center.

As Phil Smith said, in the early 1970s, there wasn't much to the area. The local landmark was a Stuckey's Pecan Shoppe alongside Interstate 4. According to Charlie Wadsworth, the shop and its manager, B.W. Clements, had to quickly pivot to selling sandwiches and coffee due to an influx of pesky real estate speculators.[15] The shop, on a triangular spit of land between the highway and the state road, backed up directly onto Disney-owned land. Stuckey either beat Disney to the punch or had an incredible stroke of luck.

Preview Center manager Bill Hoelscher recalled, "There was one guy, a Mr. Clements, and he would hold court at Stuckey's. Folks would come out to see what he was up to, and 'Mr. Stuckey' would tell everybody a bunch of misinformation. So at that time, the company thought 'hey it's a good idea. Why don't we build our own Preview Center?'"[16]

This small, unassuming building was constructed in what Disney described as "south seas modern" style and opened to the public in January 1970. Visitors passed a sign on I-4 instructing them to pull off on State Road Road 535 and then turn left. Bill Hoelscher remembered: "At that time there was not much there except Stuckey's, a pet alligator I fed regularly, and construction people."[17]

Aerial overview of the interchange of I-4 and 353 around about 1968, looking west. The roof of Stuckey's is just visible in the bottom right. Black Lake (*center*) would be renamed Lake Buena Vista. Just beyond that the Bronson airstrip and hangars are visible. The Bronson house sat just south of the hangars. The Walt Disney World Preview Center would be built on the southern shore of Black Lake. *Author's collection.*

The building itself is attractively elevated, giving sweeping views of Black Lake, a natural body of water to the north.[18] Ascending the front steps, visitors entered a reception area featuring a souvenir stand, a refreshment counter dispensing orange juice and an information desk where they could sign into a guestbook indicating their name and home state.[19]

The Preview Center itself consisted of a central cluster of offices with a perimeter gallery running around them. Floor-to-ceiling glass windows let natural light shine on concept paintings on the walls of the gallery.

Inside the core of the building was a presentation space featuring a model of Walt Disney World with a movie screen above it. A twelve-minute film was shown every fifteen minutes to crowds of up to 625 individuals. They could then take their time to peruse the outer gallery and buy a souvenir guide or a Walt Disney World license plate in the lobby.

But most importantly, the Preview Center offered the public the first taste of what Walt Disney World would finally be and offered Floridians their first taste of the famous Disney culture: vibrant colors, wholesome employees and, most importantly, thoughtful, engaging design.

Top: *Courtesy of the Orlando Public Library.*

Bottom: West gallery of the Preview Center; the theater exit was around the corner at left. *Courtesy of the Orlando Public Library.*

OK, well male visitors fixated on the "Preview Center girls." There is much contemporary newspaper ink and photo reproductions of the attractive, polite nature of the fourteen hostesses who escorted visitors around the center. After getting their fill of soda, art and pretty girls, visitors could wander the manicured landscape and enjoy the view of Lake Buena Vista from a gazebo on the shore.[20]

The Preview Center was a hit from the start. Some 3,000 visitors streamed into it on the first day—a number that defied all expectations— and they never let up. "If they can pull in crowds like this just for a movie, imagine what it'll be like when the real thing opens," one visitor told Glenn Hoffer of the *Fort Lauderdale News*.[21] The final attendance figure was some 1.3 million visitors between January 1970 and September 1971, when the center closed.[22]

And then something funny happened. Time just stood still for the Preview Center while Walt Disney World groaned with expansion all around it. It's there in a blissfully preserved state, a quirk of fate somehow extended to scarce else at Disney World. You can go there yourself, right now, and see at least the outside of it, and it looks pretty much like what people driving up in 1970 would've seen. The trees are taller, and the gazebo is gone, but the past is still there waiting for you.[23]

Take some time out of your trip, park in the parking lot, walk around the building and stand on the shores of Black Lake. Watch the reeds in the lake sway gently, strands of Spanish moss rake the ground in the breeze and birds fly overhead. The starting pistol for the mad rush of modern Florida was heard here, baptized in orange juice, fed on hype and fired by fourteen pretty girls. The state has never been the same since.

4

THE PALACE OF KING CITRUS

Not every landmark has been so dutifully preserved. From the Preview Center, let's take a short ride up Apopka-Vineland Road, past the Lake Buena Vista hospital built in 1971 (now a CentraCare), out of the bustle of the tourist strip and toward a vibrant bedroom community called Dr. Phillips. The doctor is the last of our cast of colorful characters to have had an impact on the prehistory of Walt Disney World.

Dr. Phillip Phillips wasn't a doctor, but he never let that stop him.[24] "Doc" was Orlando's first millionaire, a mercurial man who possessed a knack for marketing produce. Phillips was the first to can citrus juice and also the first to solicit doctors to advertise its health benefits. His landholdings in Florida ultimately amounted to some five thousand acres of citrus groves.

Through the 1920s, Phillips began to accumulate acreage in Orlando between Conroy Road and Sand Lake with the vision of building a workers' community of five thousand—with a schoolhouse, post office, electricity, running water and train depot. And to anchor his planned community, Doc built the largest citrus packinghouse in the United States. It was a crowning achievement.

The packinghouse opened three days before Halloween in 1928, and it was a thirty-five-thousand-square-foot behemoth. Fruit could be received from trucks on three sides and fed through machines that would automatically sort, wash, dry and individually wrap each orange, tangerine and grapefruit. The citrus was packed into white spruce boxes and stored in refrigerated rooms to await the arrival of the train. Locomotives on the

AERIAL VIEW OF PACKING HOUSE AND GROVE AT DOCTOR PHILLIPS, FLORIDA

Vintage postcard. *Author's collection.*

Atlantic Coast Line arrived on their own special spur, pulling up alongside the refrigerated rooms on the building's west side. The fruits reached market in Japanese tissue paper that had the Doc's image printed on each sheet. In the center of the packinghouse floor was an employee cafeteria, restrooms, a smoking room and lockers. A giant clock stood in the center of the production floor.

The huge curved steel structure was arc-welded, a novelty in 1928, and the interior was spray-painted in a color called "Barreled Sunlight." Behind the building was a new metal-sided mill for the manufacture of citrus fertilizer.

Back when Orlando was still a sleepy backwater of a place, the Phillips packinghouse was a modern marvel and the city's first attraction. Tourists arrived via bus to walk the mezzanine atop the cafeteria. Postcards were sold, and visitors received a "special gift."[25]

All of this greatly enhanced Orlando's claim to be the center of the citrus industry in Florida. But these times would not last. By the end of World War II, with the Doc aging out of daily work in the industry and his two sons going in separate directions, the Phillips landholdings began to be split up.

In 1954, the Phillips family sold their orange groves to Minute Maid.[26] This seems to not have included the chief landholdings on the shores of Sand Lake, which the Doc's son Howard began to develop into a planned community. This community has spread into the colorful suburb we see today.

This sale to Minute Maid definitely did include the packinghouse and surrounding groves.[27] Minute Maid, which had its own modern packinghouse across town, probably closed the historic Phillips plant, and the building exits from official record.

But, ghost-like, it still haunts Orlando. The plant was definitely still standing in 1969 as Disney was being built. In June 1968, intrepid *Fort Lauderdale News* reporter Wesley Stout drove up to see what all of the fuss was about with Disney coming to town. He turned off on 535, pulling into Stuckey's to ask directions. Mr. Clements told him to drive north about five miles. Because most of the Florida property was still untracked swamp in mid-1968, he found nothing:

> *We came to drainage and road construction, commonplace everywhere in Florida, and were not even certain this was Disney activity. Soon we found ourselves amidst one of Minute Maid's big Dr. Phillips groves. On the edge of the road was a long idle fertilizer mill, with empty sheet metal huts and a rail spur.*

Interior of the packinghouse in brighter days. *Courtesy of Orange County Regional History Center.*

Painting vinyl leaves for the Swiss
Family Treehouse inside the Phillips
fertilizer mill, 1971. *Author's collection.*

He had indeed come to Disney activity but did not recognize it. That was
by design. Bill Sullivan recalled:

> *Bud Washo had come down to build the castle and all the fiberglass
> (structures) so we rented this old orange packing warehouse....We cleared
> out the interior and made a staff shop out of it. That's where a lot of stuff
> for Magic Kingdom got built.*[28]

Under the direction of Bud Washo, the Dr. Phillips warehouse became
a de facto scenic shop for the construction activities at Disney. The large
gnarled branches of the Swiss Family Treehouse and some haunted trees
for the Haunted Mansion took shape inside,[29] as did many other large-scale
scenic elements for Magic Kingdom.[30]

As the locomotives for the Walt Disney World Railroad were completed
at the Tampa Shipyards, they were put onto an Atlantic Coast Railway
siding at the shipyards and driven up to Dr. Phillips under compressed air.
The locomotives arrived on the rail siding at the packinghouse and were
then trucked into Walt Disney World.[31] All of this makes the Dr. Phillips
packinghouse a historically significant part of Disney history, integral to the
construction effort.

And it may have been the last thing of historic significance to happen to
the packinghouse, for it vanishes from our view shortly thereafter. Minute
Maid sold the property back to the Dr. Phillips Foundation in 1973, which
turned around and sold it to Granada, which began clearing the land.[32] The

Granada subdivision "Citrus Chase" began construction on the spot in 1980 and was completed in 1984.

Today Dr. Phillips's name is remembered all across Orlando as a representative of that dim and distant day when citrus, not tourism, was king. But for just one moment, King Citrus and "King Mickey" met, in location if not in spirit, in a giant building that was the pride of Orlando in its day. And as the wheel of time turned, that meeting increasingly resembled a changing of the guard, as one monarch departed and another took its place, all in a massive half round building surrounded by millions and millions of citrus trees…once upon a time in Florida.

PART II

· ——————————————— ·

ACTION CENTER

We feel it's something like bringing in the Spindle Top oil field in Texas in 1901. We expect the same results. The economic effect has already started.

–Martin Andersen, *publisher of the* Orlando Sentinel, *1966*

5

HURRY UP AND BUILD

O ne hot day in 1965, the Orlando Chamber of Commerce announced its intention to rebrand Orlando from "The City Beautiful"—a moniker selected in 1908—to "Florida's Action Center."[33] This produced much sniggering among locals. In 1964, Orlando was a sleepy community of 230,000, described by Bill Sullivan as the "biggest small town you've ever seen." Besides citrus, the chief industry was the Martin-Marietta plant and the Space Center at Cape Kennedy, which was an hour's drive. Outside of the brand-new Interstate 4, where was the action?

But in October 1965, everything changed, and prophecy became reality. *Orlando Sentinel* reporter Emily Bavar was on a trip with several other newspaper writers to Disneyland and an exclusive lunch with Walt Disney. She remembered:

> *I was, as usual, the only woman among the writers, a fact of life I had grown accustomed to. And as the press conference opened, I silently rehearsed a question I had been reserving for Disney.*
>
> *I put the question to him and watched for his reaction—any sign that would betray him. There was none. I pursued on the grounds of being the only woman there, I was in a position to be persistent. I felt as subtle as Minnie Mouse as I bombarded this man with questions he clearly didn't wish to answer. I sat beside him at lunch and was certain I was ruining his lamb chops as I turned the conversation from Disneyland back to Central Florida, a subject on which he finally began to display amazing knowledge.*

Souvenir postcard showing some typical Florida activities in the decades before Disney's arrival. If you know what the outboard motor is doing here, please write in! *Author's collection.*

He knew the average annual rainfall, he was familiar with present and proposed highways, he knew there would be a large labor force available as work at Cape Kennedy tapered off.

When I returned to my hotel room that evening I went over my notes. He knew far more about Central Florida than many of us who have lived here most of our lives. The Central Florida acreage had to be Walt Disney's. That's what I told my editor when I called him from the Disneyland Hotel in Anaheim.[34]

And that's what we told Orlando Sentinel *readers the next morning.[35]*

The *Sentinel* ran this headline: "We Say: 'Mystery Industry' Is Disney." Disney associate William Potter was in town and picked up the newspaper at his hotel. Potter was on the phone within minutes with Walt. Disney knew he was cornered as soon as he got the news. Within weeks, Disney was in Florida confirming the report at Orlando's Cherry Plaza Hotel. Orlando was suddenly and in a very real way the "Action Center" of Florida.

Land clearing began in May 1967.[36] John Hench recalled of the barren expanse of earth: "It just looked so damn big. If we flew over it once, we flew over it a hundred times. What we were planning just seemed so minuscule compared to the landscape."[37] While the initial buildout consisting of The

Magic Kingdom, two resort hotels, two golf courses and the campground seems small compared to the sprawl and scope of modern Walt Disney World, it's easy to underestimate what an undertaking this was. Disney expected the project to consume $60 million. It ended up topping out at $400 million.

Disney had two remarkable men helping, the first of whom was Rear Admiral Joe Fowler, who had served in both world wars, designed aircraft carriers and overseen all shipyards on the West Coast of the United States during World War II. As Operations Chief Dick Nunis put it, Fowler could "uncomplicate even the most daunting challenge."[38]

Fowler was the rubber-meets-road man who got Disneyland built in under a year. He was never given anything as formal as a title—he just built. Walt met Joe through C.V. Wood and invited Fowler to come to the Disney Studio to advise on the construction of the Mark Twain Riverboat. Believing he was going on a day trip, Fowler brought a single change of clothes. After getting a thirty-minute brief from Walt Disney, Fowler was summarily escorted to an

Riles Island still slumbers peacefully as the Vacation Kingdom of the World rises just behind, mid-1971. *Courtesy of the Orlando Public Library.*

office, handed the keys to a car and introduced to construction contractors to begin negotiations. He didn't return home for three weeks.[39]

During construction of Walt Disney World, Joe Fowler was somehow simultaneously the senior vice president of engineering and construction, a member of the board of directors and headed up the Buena Vista Construction Company.

If that wasn't enough, Disney also absorbed William E. "Joe" Potter, who had come into contact with Walt Disney through the 1964 New York World's Fair. A West Point graduate from Wisconsin, Potter had helped plan D-Day and served as governor of the Panama Canal Zone. The 1964 World's Fair was a disaster for almost everyone involved—Six Flags Over Texas builder Angus Wynne went bankrupt trying to operate his seven (!) Texas pavilions—and Joe Potter jumped ship to Disney.[40]

Potter oversaw the planning of the property's infrastructure, an invisible but brilliant piece of engineering amounting to a $20 million investment. The easy way to remember this is that Potter prepared the land for construction and Fowler built on it.

One of Disney's initial challenges was to regulate the flow of water across the land. In Florida, you have to build runoff areas for the incredible amount of rainfall the area receives; locals call these "retention ponds." They are basically glorified puddles.

Potter connected all of the property's natural bodies of water—Black Lake, Bay Lake and Reedy Creek—with drainage canals.

> Our system was based primarily on being able to let floods through a system of automatic gates, which would shut as soon as the flood had passed. Through the use of these gates, we were able to keep the ground water at a level that it had before so that the root systems of trees would think that things were just as normal as they always had been.[41]

As Dick Nunis pointed out in his autobiography, Walt Disney World has never had to close due to flooding.

Additionally, the land selected for the construction of the theme park proved to be too swampy to be practical. Joe Potter moved the theme park north, and property art director Bill Martin filled the empty spot with the Seven Seas Lagoon. The park was built above ground level; an undulating series of basements would allow out-of-sight transit of employees, vehicles, dumpsters and trash compactors. All of these tunnel networks were then buried in the earth excavated for the Seven Seas Lagoon, atop which The

Before there was Disney World or even Six Gun Territory, Central Florida's premier attraction was Cypress Gardens. The brainchild of Dick Pope, the attraction featured southern belles, abundant flora and water skiing. On October 29, 1969, Cypress Gardens premiered its "Chatterbox." This tiny hexagonal building was situated on the shores of Lake Eloise and was a luxuriously carpeted and air-conditioned phone booth operated by push button. It was essentially a Tomorrowland exhibit for land lines.

Its unveiling was a milestone for Central Florida, as this represented the 750,000th telephone in Central Florida. This number must have seemed colossal in 1969. Its unveiling also looked ahead to another milestone, because the very first call placed was from Dick Pope to Roy Disney, who exchanged pleasantries about the weather. Also on hand was Fred D. Learey, president of General Telephone Corporation. He commented: "Since tourism has played such an important role in the growth of this area, it is fitting that this special booth be placed in Cypress Gardens, probably one of the most famous attractions in the world." Presumably, Roy Disney returned their call moments later to inform them that they hadn't seen nothing yet!

Joe Fowler points to the cleared spot where Magic Kingdom will be built. A balloon with mouse ears marks the location of Cinderella Castle. *Courtesy of the Orlando Public Library.*

Magic Kingdom was built. When you disembark the monorail and enter the park, you are actually standing on the roof of a massive building. This pushes Cinderella Castle up above the natural tree line, where it appears to float dreamily on the horizon, even after fifty years of growth.

Disney chose California firm J.B. Allen, which built the Submarine Lagoon and Matterhorn at Disneyland,[42] to oversee the project. Allen knew it was drowning in the work from the jump. Construction lagged and lagged, spurred by the lackadaisical pace of the unionized workers and Disney's perfectionist art directors. Disney made crews tear down the steel canopy over the Carrousel in Fantasyland and rebuild it because it was two inches off spec.[43]

The J.B. Allen and Disney people missed Coors, which was then only sold west of the Rockies. Operations Manager Ron Heminger took matters into his own hands by taking up a collection to drive out a hoard of Coors inside a load of materials destined for Peter Pan's Flight. The beer was inside a container labeled "Small Tools and Parts."[44] Elsewhere on the site, materials and tools were stolen constantly, and at least once an outhouse behind Main Street was set ablaze.

Local journalist Edward Prizer was given a tour of the construction on the Contemporary Resort in mid-1971. He captures with epic aplomb the mad rush to meet opening day:

> *The rat-a-tat of rivet guns rips the air. Steel clangs against steel. Monstrous trucks grind through the mud. An asphalt machine emits the pungent scent of tar. Entering the hotel by the service door, we find ourselves in a concrete crypt swarming with workmen in hardhats. The lights are dim. Pools of muddy water eddy across the concrete floor. A maze of pipes and conduits and metal ducts hang from walls and ceiling.*

A dozen workmen are waiting for the elevator. The plywood door slides back and the elevator gaps open. The box is jammed with our bodies. The faces are grimly businesslike or just plain wary in the faded light of a single overhead bulb.[45]

It became evident that J.B. Allen was simply not going to finish on time, so Fowler fired the firm and formed his own construction company, Buena Vista Construction, in one hurried weekend. Meantime, Disneyland Operations president Dick Nunis—a legendary hard-ass—was flown in to ride herd on the effort. He left strict instructions in California: "When I call, don't say 'when'—it means yesterday."[46]

Nunis paced around the property, dictating a constant stream of updates to California via tape recorder and sleeping in the few finished hotel rooms. When he saw construction crews lagging, Nunis jumped right in and began to do the work himself or bribed crews with cases of beer. The overtime—and paychecks—grew proportionally.

In the end, the park crossed the finish line on time—barely. Just as at Disneyland in 1955, most of the shop interiors and all of Tomorrowland were still to be built. 20,000 Leagues Under the Sea in Fantasyland would not open until December due to a delay in the arrival of the submarines. The Contemporary had a crane hanging over it until well into 1972. The hotel's lawn had been sodded the night before, with Nunis pressing every

"Utilidor" beneath Cinderella Castle takes shape. *Courtesy of the Orlando Public Library.*

41

able-bodied person in the management team into serving, standing before them and bellowing, "Come on, guys, you can do it! Green side up!" Nunis recalled:

> *Before we even finished, we saw we weren't going to have enough sod. [Landscaper] Bill Evans drew a big circle out front and said "we'll leave this bare. People will think it's a planter." Guests walked around the circled area as if it had been planned that way.*[47]

Disney intentionally chose a Friday in October as a slow day to begin the opening process. Orlandoans breathed a sigh of relief that the projected car pileup to the Georgia border did not materialize. By Thanksgiving, the project had been deemed a success. Roy O. Disney died in December. And then the real work began.

The little world unto itself was in orbit. But it was a world inside of a world, and just as drastically as Disney had transformed "the sorriest piece of land around," Disney would change Orlando forever.

6

ORLANDO'S U.S. STEEL STORY

U.S. Steel was formed in 1901 by J.P. Morgan out of assets merged together from Andrew Carnegie and two other steel producers. At the height of its power, U.S. Steel controlled two-thirds of the steel produced in the United States and was the world's first billion-dollar company.

In March 1969, with fingers already in the pies of mining, materials, refining, agriculture, engineering and construction financing, U.S. Steel announced the formation of U.S. Steel Realty to develop uses for all of its industrial might and raw materials.[48] This amounted to a vertical monopoly, with U.S. Steel trucks delivering product and materials made in U.S. Steel plants to build U.S. Steel houses financed by U.S. Steel.

The company announced—what else—a planned community called Belleaire outside Clearwater, Florida, and a variety of industrial park projects. And in May 1969, USS Realty announced its splashy debut project: construction of the Polynesian and Contemporary Resorts at Walt Disney World using its revolutionary "unitized" construction technique.

> *In unitized construction, each hotel room is assembled at ground level in an on-site facility designed for this purpose. Furnishings and basic utilities including bathrooms and air-conditioning are installed and the door locked. Then the room is hoisted into place, and the utilities "plugged in." Disney planners point out that it is possible, because the room will be so complete when hoisted into place, that "the first person entering the room after it leaves the factory could be the maid."*[49]

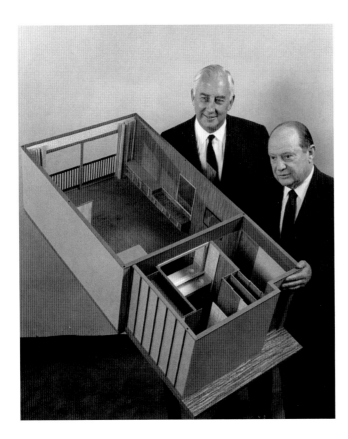

U.S. Steel representatives with a model of one of the company's modular hotel rooms. *Courtesy of the Orlando Public Library.*

To effect this plan, a factory operated by U.S. Steel subsidiary American Bridge Company was constructed a few miles away from the site of the Contemporary. Inside the L-shaped factory, hotel room units were framed up, wired and fitted with pipes and fixtures, all the while progressing from the rear of the *L*-shaped factory to the loading bays in twenty-six stops. Upon completion, they were delivered via flatbed truck and lifted into a steel mesh network to be connected to utilities. This factory could produce about forty rooms a week.[50] Orlando journalist Edward Prizer described seeing "a crew of men squirting a fireproof substance on a big brown box— another room for the hotel." U.S. Steel estimated that this new technique would "save months."[51]

The first four rooms to come off the assembly line, however, were not destined for Walt Disney World. U.S. Steel hauled them a dozen miles up Apopka-Vineland Road to Bay Hill, a golf community built on former Dr. Phillips groves along the shores of Lake Tibet. These four rooms were arranged around a courtyard and were then all covered over to become what U.S. Steel described disingenuously as "a cottage." In reality, this was a corporate clubhouse with a sleek covered atrium. Disney used the U.S. Steel "cottage" to woo corporate sponsors, and this was probably the site of many a deal signed in 1970 and 1971.

This spirit of bonhomie between the two companies concealed the fact that U.S. Steel was getting in deeper and deeper water. Its intent was to use the splashy Disney World project to sell the world on the merits of "unitized" construction, and it intended apartments, houses and classrooms to begin spilling forth from the Bay Lake factory on Disney World's glorious opening. In reality, construction was falling behind schedule, and U.S. Steel knew that the 1,500 hotel rooms would never be ready on time. Given that Disney had already fired J.B. Allen, the writing was on the wall.

One detail that is often forgotten in subsequent histories is that U.S. Steel expected to own the Contemporary and Polynesian; Disney was going to lease the hotels and operate them. A commercial for the Contemporary that aired during the Grand Opening of Walt Disney World television special confidently purrs, "U.S. Steel owns this specular spectacular hotel." We can only speculate how differently the history of Walt Disney World would have turned out had this come true.

The whole reason Disney struck the deal with U.S. Steel in the first place was to defer construction costs, which had already ballooned to $400 million. But Roy Disney, almost always the canniest guy in the room, recognized that the partnership was doomed to fail. He called Donn Tatum before his desk and told him he wanted to buy out the U.S. Steel interests. "I'm doing you a favor—we're not going to be good partners with them."[52]

The $90 million buyout was completed on December 21, 1971—one day after Roy's death. It was that deal that set Disney on the course to become the corporate leviathan it is today.

Disney's hotels wrapped up construction in early 1972. Just as Roy had predicted, the partnership with U.S. Steel had gone sour. In order to produce truly ready-made hotel rooms, Disney had to make some odd design choices for the room interiors. The main piece of furniture was a large dresser attached to the left-hand wall, containing drawers and a built-in television. The sole freestanding table was bolted to the floor in the rear of the room; the bed also was affixed to its wall. Lighting was entirely built into the ceiling; various lighting "modes" could be selected from a panel on the wall. It was innovative and sleek, and everyone really hated it.

Furthermore, the rooms in the Contemporary and Polynesian were almost identical. Disney wasn't certain if people would want themed decor

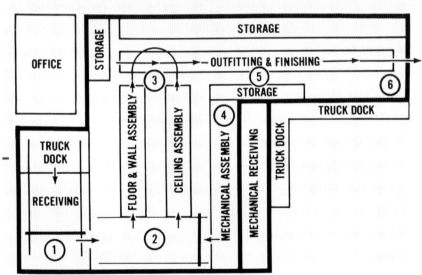

This page: Aerial photo and diagram showing the U.S. Steel "unitized construction" plant. Notice all of the assembled hotel rooms sitting outside in the sun. *Courtesy of the Orlando Public Library.*

inside their rooms or not; it turned out they did. Very quickly, wallpaper, framed prints and floral bedspreads were added to make the rooms look more welcoming.

In 1972, U.S. Steel produced 816 hotel rooms for the Court of Flags motel before throwing in the towel and selling the plant to Disney. Nowhere was it noted at the time this connection; most newspapers simply stated the rooms were built by "American Bridge." The cost savings of united construction turned out to be in theory only. U.S. Steel attempted to move the whole operation to Clearwater to construct its Belleaire community, but that factory closed, too.[53]

U.S. Steel sold the "cottage" in 1975,[54] signaling the company's departure in defeat from the Central Florida scene. In a strange postscript, the cottage came to national attention in the fall of 1976 during the presidential race between Jimmy Carter and Gerald Ford. The Federal Securities and Exchange Commission reported that U.S. Steel may had paid for golfing outings for Ford in exchange for kickbacks. These scandals were concurrent with—although not necessarily a cause of—Ford's slip in the polling behind Carter.

Today, the original Disney hotel rooms built by American Bridge are totally unrecognizable, and many have been knocked through and reformatted into different room shapes. The Court of Flags Hotel sat inside Florida Center and was torn down in 2006. Today it's the location of a Lexus dealership.

The U.S. Steel cottage still stands today alongside the sixteenth hole in Bay Hill. After passing through a few corporate owners, it was converted into a residence in 1980. I wonder if the people who live there know anything about its history or the deals and scandals that took place within its walls.

7

JOHNNY'S CORNER

Everything from Snuff to Eggs

Because access to the Disney construction site was heavily regulated, newspaper reporters across Florida looked for any alternative to report on what was then the world's largest private construction project. By chance, an opportunity presented itself just outside of the property. Construction crews had descended on Johnny's Corner, a sleepy little country store on Disney's front doorstep. The transformation was remarkable.

"At Johnny's Corner a man can get pig knuckles with his beer, a fan belt for his car, a can of snuff, a pair of used socks, a Barlow knife, or a Hong Kong suit 'made to measure' for $49. He can cuss loud, peel eggs, play pin ball, argue about the Union, eat sardines out of the can and hand wrestle by the gas pumps."[55] He could also, most importantly, cash those huge overtime Disney paychecks.

Johnny's Corner got its start as Jock's Happy Corner, opening in 1949 and owned by Jock and Fern Lowery. This was a stone's throw away from the Bronson family compound with its airstrip and ranch house that Phil Smith ended up living in. In an April 23, 2010 *Orlando Sentinel* article commemorating Fern Lowery, her daughter remembered: "It was nothing but orange groves back then. Our house was built onto the back of the store, so if people needed gas or something at any hour of the night, Momma or Daddy would wake up to help them."

The Disney announcement and subsequent rush of land speculators changed Jock's Happy Corner forever. Local politicians and businesses celebrated, then panicked. Crime would rise—their yearly budget for law and order would triple. They'd need to build a jail and courthouse on Disney's front door. Unwanted pregnancies would quadruple. Hippies were already lounging around in Lake Eola Park. The *Orlando Sentinel* republished articles from the *Anaheim Bulletin* reporting on the gridlock of cars resulting from the opening of Disneyland.

With business at Stuckey's picking up rapidly and the pace of the work only escalating, Jock and Fern sent themselves off to an early retirement by selling the business to Johnny Speakman in 1967, who rechristened the old store Johnny's Corner. Johnny was a genuine Florida old-timer, and he must have decided the payout wasn't worth the work because he sold out to Bill Waring and Bob Morgan after two years of frenzy. By the time United Press reporter David Langford arrived in November 1970, the place was a veritable zoo:

> *Except for a few orange pickers in season, the customers at Johnny's Corner are brawny men with Mickey Mouse decals on their hard hats. They are the working men who are not allowed in the executive cafeteria at the Disney site about a "country mile" away. At noon they bring their lunch boxes and sit at two big wooden tables. They buy milk in half-quart cartons, Gatorade in pop top cans, pies, hot sausages, potato chips and bean dip. But at quitting time it's beer they're after. Lots of beer.*
>
> *"On a pay day we'll sell as much as 50 cases," said Bob Morgan, Waring's partner. "You can safely say it's one of the best beer accounts in Orange County."*
>
> *That's of little surprise. More than 2,500 workers are already on the job at the "Magic Kingdom," a short distance down State Road 535, and the number is growing. It's the largest private construction project underway in the United States. Waring, 40, and Morgan, 55, sleep during the week at the rear of the store. They get up at 4 a.m. to start the coffee and after closing they boil and pickle eggs—"about 20 dozen a week."*
>
> *"We spice them up with hot pepper and garlic sauce or anything else that we can find and man, you can't keep them on the counter," Waring says.*
>
> *"I sold a man a pair of my own pants last week." Waring said, "A man came in here not long ago who had forgot his socks. I don't know how he managed to do that but I went and got an old pair I had and sold that to him for a dollar."*

British journalist Alan Whicker stopped by to film the scene for British television. With Bill and Bob in the foreground, the parking lot of the tiny

Johnny's Corner in 1971. *Author's collection.*

place looks so busy that there's no way to wedge any one of those '60s Detroit gas guzzlers in on its edge.

The spectacle drove home the deal with the devil that Orlando had made. A movie studio arriving in town and building a billion-dollar wonderland is abstract for the average resident, but this free-for-all of commerce was understandable—human scale. Johnny's Corner became a focal point for the ugly side of the earliest years of Walt Disney World, before it was even really a thing that existed—piles of concrete, dirt, cement and steel framing. It's easy to see why the residents of surrounding communities looked on in horror. What would become of *their* towns?

And Johnny's Corner became emblematic of the fate that awaited Orlando in another sense. The June 1971 issue of *News from Walt Disney World*, the company's official newsletter for the families of construction crews, simply stated: "What happened to Johnny's Corner? Progress took its toll and that historic landmark was demolished to make way for a modern service station."

Which is true and also—not. Johnny's Corner continued to sell cigarettes and beer, but not in the original location. Bill Waring and Bob Morgan sold the property and closed in June 1971—then moved three hundred feet across the street. Reopening in October 1971 as Johnny's Country Store, Bill

In 1968, Disney purchased land in Bay Hill and constructed five identical two-bedroom "cottages" for use by the Disney executive team. These served as a base of operations for the construction effort, with Roy Disney's house and Joe Fowler's house sharing a driveway. Roy's Cottage was the location of a gala backyard barbecue on the evening of April 30, 1969. Press and politicians gathered to celebrate Walt Disney World Preview Day, the event where the initial attractions and 1971 opening day were announced.

Following Roy's death, Disney maintained these five cottages as an executive retreat for thirty years, finally selling them to the Bay Lake Club in 2000. They still exist today in renovated form, and amazingly enough, you can rent them. For those of you wishing to party like Roy O. Disney with your own backyard barbecue, the cottage to request is number 8922.

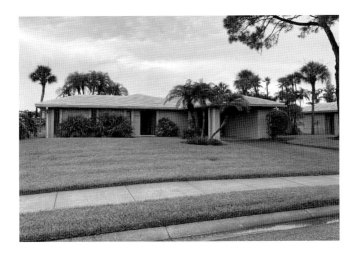

and Bob continued their boom business.[56] The scene repeated itself with the construction of EPCOT Center ten years later.

Today, the intersection that once was Johnny's Corner houses a Shell service station and a strip mall that features the Dragon Super Buffet. Across the street where once Bill Waring and Bob Morgan had their second version of Johnny's Corner stands a Miller Ale House, where cast members still go to get drunk. As far as I know, they won't sell you pants.

8

Oblivion Airlines
and the Singing Runway

The trouble with Florida is there's just too darn much of it. The state is massive, spread out, and there's not a lot between points.

This is true even in the crowded Floridian twenty-first century, but it's been a problem for as long as Floridians have been sweaty. Tallahassee was constructed as the state capital halfway between Pensacola and Jacksonville as a compromise. Live in Daytona Beach and want to drive to Miami for the weekend? It's a long drive with almost nothing worth seeing along the way. Live over by Naples or Fort Myers and want to do the same? You may be better off flying.

Flying…that's an idea. At least that's what Floridians in the 1960s thought, living in a state noteworthy for empty land and huge gaps between civilization. What if we could just *fly* to Miami?

The concept for an aircraft meant exclusively for "location hopping" flights was by no means a new one, but it was undergoing a bit of a renaissance in the 1960s. Multiple companies were developing STOL—Short TakeOff and Landing—planes throughout this era.

The Department of Defense was interested in moving troops into battle areas with such a plane, and so Lockheed-Martin was building one. Elsewhere, Congress had been funding a project to develop a plane that could take off and land vertically—VSTOL—since 1953. All of this was priming the pump for interest in civilian uses of these technologies.

This is because the size of airplanes had grown tremendously after World War II, meaning the size of the runways they required had multiplied as

Applicants wait in line outside of the Walt Disney World employment office in early 1971. *Author's collection.*

well. Airports built during the initial frenzy of excitement for air travel in the 1920s could no longer accommodate these new superjets, and commercial air travel was still so expensive that many cities were not yet certain they were ready to spend on the new runways. Orlando was among these fence-sitters. The Orlando Municipal Airport[57] was simply too small to serve major carriers. Another airport in Kissimmee was seen as too remote. In these days, it wasn't uncommon to get to Orlando by flying into Jacksonville or Miami and taking a train. Meanwhile, congestion grew at the nation's jetports.

Then in November 1968, the FAA announced that the United States needed to build at least *eight hundred* new airports to relieve current gridlock and officially recommended that STOL aircraft be considered for heavily congested areas. This seems to have been the compromise solution that many medium-sized cities were waiting to hear. LaGuardia, JFK and Newark had been testing STOLports since August. Across the country, Los Angeles Airlines was hopping between LAX and smaller landing strips within a sixty-mile radius at the same time. All of this looked so promising that the City of New York developed plans to build a STOLport on top of the Hudson River between 26th and 33rd Streets—Midtown Manhattan.

All of this sounds tremendously exciting, but there's a catch. Nobody had actually built a viable STOL plane yet—most operators were flying DeHavilland Twin Otters, a model that was ten years old and provided limited passenger volume. For any of this to be commercially viable, somebody had to come up with a STOL vehicle that could move around one hundred passengers. Municipalities were looking to build runways for planes that didn't exist. They were trying to build the plane while they were flying it.

In September 1970, Eastern Airlines, based in Miami, announced that it intended on transforming Florida into the nation's next major market for STOL flights. Eastern was developing its own STOL plane and a connecting network of STOLports across Florida.[58] All of this was occurring as a backdrop for the construction of Walt Disney World, and area residents and politicians were breaking out in hives at the perceived traffic apocalypse that would shortly consume Orlando. Sam Roen, writing for *Orlandoland Magazine* in November 1971, recalled these fears:

> *Before Disney World opened, everyone had a certain percentage of fright in their system about all of the terrible things that were going to happen—the food stores were going to run out of food, the electric power was going to break down, the water supply was going to give out and traffic was going to be backed up to Long Island or the Georgia state line at least.*

Disney repeatedly attempted to assuage these fears by stating that the highway system was "more than adequate to meet their needs." Still, Orlando didn't really have a jetport—where exactly were these tourists supposed to fly into? On July 1970, Disney confirmed that it was in talks with "an Orlando-based supplemental airline." "There have been a lot of advances on the STOL and the VSTOL and they have been introduced elsewhere on a practical basis," said a Disney World spokesman. He emphasized, however, that these dealings with the Orlando airline were in the talking and thinking stage and no decision had been made.[59]

Meanwhile, every major airport in the area was jumping up and down for a piece of the tourism pie. Melbourne, moderately closer to Orlando than Tampa, talked about building a STOLport to fly directly to Disney's

ASSEMBLING A GIANT WORLD — Looking south at the theme park — across the lagoon, resort hotel sites and the parking lot — here's where the major components of Walt Disney World stand today: 1) "Magic Kingdom" theme park attractions are well along. Cinderella's Castle still rising to eventual 18-story height, buildings up for "Haunted Mansion," "It's A Small World," and the Fantasyland dark rides. Sub lagoon excavated, Rivers of America and Jungle Cruise channels excavated, and Swiss Tree still going up. Construction started on Liberty Square and soon on Great Ceremonial House. Basement excavated for Tomorrowland, facades going up on all Main Street shops. 2) "Magic Kingdom" Entrance — Docks and break water nearly complete, monorail station foundations finished. 3) Contemporary Hotel Site — 14-story elevator shaft nearly complete, modular hotel units going up for low-rise annex, Bay Lake dock erected. 4) Venetian Hotel Site preparation complete, landscaping begun. 5) Parking lot for 14,000 day guests cleared and planted with Eucalyptus trees. 6) Main entrance boulevard connecting SR 530 and Phase I area paving begun. 7) Polynesian Hotel foundations started. Actual construction on 500-plus room village resort begins soon. 8) Golf course contouring completed — lagoons under excavation. Two 18-hole courses to be ready opening day. 9) Asian hotel site prepared and landscaped.

State of the "Vacation Kingdom" in about late 1970. *Author's collection.*

runway.[60] The only place in Orlando where it was feasible to land jets was McCoy Airbase, which had been hastily retrofitted into McCoy Jetport.

In the end, Disney paired with Shawnee and Executive Airlines, and the service began on October 23, 1971, with the opening of the Lake Buena Vista STOLport. Disney flew in five Florida mayors: David Kennedy of Miami, Jay Dermer of Miami Beach, Frank Foster Jr. of West Palm Beach, James Levitt of Fort Lauderdale and Carl Langford of Orlando. The flight from downtown Orlando must have been spectacular, flying over the low ranch homes, past the lakes and orange groves, then turning past Cinderella Castle and circling to land. Carl Langford, who was sort of a weirdo, called the route "Oblivion Airlines."[61]

On the ground, Florida secretary of transportation Ed Mueller presented Florida's first official STOLport license to Disney president Donn Tatum. Tatum remarked, "The Disney organization is privileged to be part of this experiment which will establish the feasibility of this service." And that, friends, was about as far as things ever got.

Alright, let's back this STOL plane up a bit and think about this for a moment. All of this sounds very high-toned and progressive, but the other side of this story is that Disney and Eastern were already in bed together. The Eastern-Disney alliance was announced in September 1970, the same month that Eastern made its pronouncement that it was developing a network of STOLports across Florida. Television commercials were broadcast nationwide in 1971 and 1972 promising the Eastern "whisperliners" were ready to fly you to Walt Disney World on the resort's official airline. Disney's charter with the State of Florida granted the company the ability to build its own airport if it chose, and connecting these dots, it seems clear that Eastern wanted first dibs on exclusive use of this far-future airport.

Meanwhile, Shawnee Airlines, based in Orlando and founded by David Latham, had ties to the Florida citrus industry, another Florida industry that Disney was in deep with. This is not to indicate that there was some massive conspiracy that Disney was a part of, simply to show that everyone had a good profit motive to go along with this scheme.

But the whole problem with the STOL plan was that the entire industry had to be built up at once—people who wanted to build STOL planes had to get STOL services running before it was even feasible to start manufacturing the planes to fly passengers. The whole thing was an economic form of "Who's On First?"

And the idea proved to not be all that feasible. Shawnee Airlines was promising the City of Orlando it could be the commuter plane capital of Florida in April 1972, and it folded in December 1972. The problem was the sudden influx of major carriers spurred by the opening of Walt Disney World itself. "You just can't run a Beechcraft 99 against jets," David Latham said to the *Miami Herald*. "We can't compete and neither can any other airline. It's going to take government subsidy."[62] Disney sanguinely commented to the *Miami Herald* that the loss of the air service "would have no significant effect on attendance." Ouch.

So in the end, Disney's airstrip was useful for about fourteen months. I actually can't find too much evidence that it was ever used all that frequently. I also can't find much evidence that Eastern's STOL plans ever got any further than their splashy announcement. The lack of air-conditioning on the Beechcraft planes must not have helped; pilots called them "flying locker rooms." STOL flights were the Laserdiscs of the aviation world.

But! If you know anything at all about the Lake Buena Vista STOLport, it has nothing to do with any of this political and economic drama. It's because the STOLport is the world-famous "Singing Runway." Grooves cut into the pavement meant that, if you drove across them at exactly the

STOLport FLIGHTS

Shawnee Airlines operates 11 flights daily to and from the Walt Disney World STOLport (Short Take Off and Landing). Schedule is as follows:

Departs From:	Time	Flight No.	Arrives Walt Disney World
Daytona Beach	7:55 am	71	8:45 am
Orlando-Herndon	8:30 am	71	8:45 am
Fort Lauderdale	8:30 am	78	10:00 am
Palm Beach International	9:00 am	78	10:00 am
Tampa	9:35 am	72	10:05 am
McCoy Jetport	11:30 am	51	11:45 am
McCoy Jetport	12:30 am	53	12:45 pm
McCoy Jetport	2:05 pm	55	2:20 pm
McCoy Jetport	3:50 pm	57	4:05 pm
Orlando-Herndon	4:30 pm	73	4:45 pm
McCoy Jetport	5:20 pm	59	5:35 pm
McCoy Jetport	6:10 pm	61	6:25 pm
Tampa	7:00 pm	74	7:30 pm

Departs To:	Time	Flight No.	Arrives
Tampa	8:50 am	71	9:20 am
Orlando-Herndon	10:10 am	72	10:25 am
McCoy Jetport	11:05 am	52	11:20 am
McCoy Jetport	12:05 pm	56	12:20 pm
McCoy Jetport	1:35 pm	58	1:50 pm
McCoy Jetport	3:25 pm	60	3:40 pm
McCoy Jetport	4:45 pm	62	5:00 pm
McCoy Jetport	5:45 pm	64	6:00 pm
Tampa	6:00 pm	75	6:30 pm
Palm Beach International	6:30 pm	79	7:30 pm
Fort Lauderdale	6:30 pm	79	7:55 pm
Orlando-Herndon	7:35 pm	74	7:50 pm
Daytona Beach	7:35 pm	74	8:20 pm

Courtesy of the Lake Buena Vista Historical Society.

right speed, the vibrations inside your car would play "When You Wish Upon a Star"—at least, that's the story.[63]

So, here's the thing. I drove the Singing Runway in 2003, back when at least some of it still existed. And I can report, yes, there were grooves in the pavement and they did, kind of, play something that sounded somewhat like "When You Wish Upon a Star" when driven across at about forty-five miles per hour. I've watched videos of similar singing roads in California and New Mexico and can say that both of those newer examples sounded way better than what I experienced in 2003.

Subsequent online claims seem to have conflated the use of this runway for STOL flights and the use of this runway as a weird grooved pavement experiment, claiming that the strips were intended as a "surprise" for landing planes. Thing is, I can find no mention of the grooves in any contemporary accounts of the Lake Buena Vista STOLport when it was in use, and that seems like the sort of clever touch that people would remark on. Based on that and my firsthand experience, I can say with confidence that the grooves on the runway were installed at some later date and that the experiment was probably not deemed successful. The reason why is obvious in hindsight: for the gag to work at all, the grooves must be in perfect condition, but the mere

Courtesy of Mike Lee.

fact of being recessed into roads means they are constantly being worn down by tires. The out-of-pitch vibrations I heard in 2003 were the result of years of neglect.

The Lake Buena Vista STOLport still exists today, in some senses. Back when I drove on it, all you had to do was know where to turn and drive around a few parked buses. Today the area is fenced off permanently because it's been turned into a cluster of offices and storages. The grooved pavement has been removed, and much of the rest of the runway is covered with shipping containers. Disney has even built landscaped hills to make it harder to spot from the main road.

But everyone who works at Walt Disney World still refers to the area as the STOLport, a distant echo of a time when the dream of flying directly into Walt Disney World in a plane that took off vertically like a helicopter seemed just around the corner.

9

The Rising Tide That Sank All Ships

They seem to be totally making this into a strip mall kind of town.
—*Less Than Jake, "City of Gainesville"*

A s the STOLport story demonstrates, Florida has always aggressively pursued development. Historically, this has worked out. Building railroads to nowhere in the 1890s made possible the Gold Coast of Miami, Fort Lauderdale and Key West. Building massive superhighways in the 1960s attracted highway superfan Walt Disney to the area. But there is a downside to overdevelopment, a downside any Florida resident knows painfully well.

So as a bit of counter-programming to all of this rosy Orlando development boosterism, let's take a look at just a few of the harebrained fantasy projects that Walt Disney World pulled into the orbit of Orlando. Not everyone can be a Sea World, and these are just a few of the losers in the Disney World lottery that everyone was playing in the go-go late '60s.

Let's begin with Carolando, planned for the east side of the intersection of I-4 and 192. This venture began as a merger between Diversified Food Systems[64] and Regency Square, a landholding company. The resulting entity, Carolando, naturally set about making its mark on Orlando by building a massive hotel complex named after, um, itself?

The *Orlando Sentinel* shared the breathlessly planned details at the project's announcement in 1971: a twenty-two-story hotel, convention space and, for some reason, a sixty-five-story tower patterned after the Seattle Space Needle. Nobody seemed to question what a company that built burger restaurants was doing building a 650-foot tower on Disney's front doorstep. The fact that this loopy premise even attracted investment money really shows just how hot and hopping the real estate market in Orlando was at the time.

What was actually built was, of course, the "motor lodge" hotel, consisting of 960 rooms arranged in four irregular little figure-eight shapes. A central lobby complex contained four restaurants: Limey Jim's,[65] Gatsby's Burgery, The Beef Block and the Bicycle Buffet. Despite jovial claims on the part of Carolando that it absolutely could fill all of the rooms, the rooms remained unfilled, and Carolando Corp defaulted on a $40 million loan. The complex was purchased by Hyatt.

That very same year, CBS did a report on Central Florida's development boom. As the camera panned across Carolando, Walter Cronkite's dulcet voice intoned that the area "looks like Guam right after the Japanese finished with it."[66]

In the end, Hyatt made a good go of it even without a 650-foot tower, finally closing down the hotel in the tourism bust of the early 2000s. It changed owners multiple times and now sits abandoned and awaiting demolition a mere stone's throw away from the front entrance to Disney's planned town Celebration.

Okay, even without a 650-foot tower, it's hard to call something that lasted until 2003 a failure, but we're just getting started. Let's travel up I-4 a few miles and take a look at Florida Center—"The Crossroads of Florida."

This area, surrounding the intersection of I-4 and the Florida Turnpike, was a hotspot for daydreams of riches even before Disney came to town. The company that thought it could actually turn dreams into cash was Major Realty, a Miami firm headed by R.F. Raidle.

Thanks to aggressive petitioning, in 1968, Orlando annexed the entirety of the Turkey Lake Ranch owned by Major, increasing the size of the city

Carolando after its buyout by Hyatt House. Vintage postcard. *Author's collection.*

25 percent overnight. By November 1968, Major was promising a "Florida Mall" (not that one), a Houston Astrodome, 4,000 apartments, an 800-room hotel and a 1,500-room motel for their "city of the future" now called the "Major Center."

By the time earth moving began in 1969, expectations had ballooned all out of proportion. Major Realty was now claiming the initial buildout of apartments and houses would compromise "5 to 17 percent of the community," which was projected to reach 140,000 people within fifteen years.[67] The *Orlando Evening Star*, the *Sentinel's* lifestyle-oriented weekend edition, published an article in November 1970 that reads exactly like the advertising puff piece it is. "The Major Development in Orlando" now promises "five villages," each comprising two communities with a shared "commercial center." The article goes on:

> *Every facet of living will be provided in Major Center—residential units, offices, shopping areas, service and support facilities. Recreation, education and entertainment will be available within the center too, along with any other goods, services, or facilities necessary to exist in a pleasant community 24 hours a day, seven days a week.*

The article ended with the eyebrow-raising comment that "R.F. Raidle has frequently said that Disney enables Major Center to be 'the world's greatest parasite.'" Inspiring?!

The opening of Disney World came and went in 1971. What was previously being billed with great pomp and circumstance as "a total amenity community" had now been downgraded to "one of the most important tourist accommodation centers in the entire state."[68] The planned fifteen-year population had seen a corresponding drop to a projected eighty-five thousand.

Major Center was going nowhere fast, so in August 1972 its name was changed to Florida Center.[69] By mid-1973, Major Realty had built a "modern office complex," conspicuously occupied entirely by…Major Realty. This was announced to be the start of a "33 acre executive park." By 1973, it was clear to everyone that the building boom started by Disney would in no way continue to be viable moving forward. D.M. "Mike" Miller, who worked in construction, recalled in his memoir:

> *Partly built apartment, condominium, and hotel buildings stood abandoned in receivership all around Orlando. Reinforcing bars and structural steel rusted in the Florida sun on building shells that would never be completed.*

There were hotels and motels in Lake Buena Vista, sprawling all along US 192 west of Kissimmee, and in Winter Garden. Vacancy rates were the highest in the country, in the 70% range....Orlando and Florida were gripped in the worst recession since the 1930s.

By late 1973, Major Realty threw in the towel and acknowledged that the future of its Turkey Lake Ranch holdings did not lay in city planning by announcing the development of a $500,000 Tourist Information Center. This opened with great fanfare and tethered balloon in 1974, managed by the Orlando Chamber of Commerce. Understandably, much was made in local papers of the fact that this was operated entirely without the benefit of taxpayer money.

It's hard to know what Major was thinking. The information center was located in such a way to be impossible to see from the highway, totally defeating its purpose. The building lasted mere months in its intended role. The *Sentinel* announced: "A bust as a tourist information center, the 18,000 square foot facility is a white whale waiting for a good idea. [Major Realty] has entertained proposals from four firms that would like to purchase or lease the facility and convert it into a penny arcade, an antique car show, a museum or an ice-skating rink."

In 1974, the Tourist Information Center became Mystery Fun House, an attraction almost as iconic as Disney or Sea World for Orlando visitors through the '70s and '80s. Today, the Major Realty land site is just another unremarkable area of Orlando—condos, houses, gas stations and a cluster of hotels situated just outside Universal Orlando. Major Boulevard runs directly into the Universal Campus. The site across the Turnpike, once planned for a 140,000-person "city of the future," is the site of the Orlando Outlet Malls.

In approaching our final story, we can begin, ironically enough, with Disneyland in 1955. Having just opened his personal time machine to wild success, Walt Disney decided that next he wanted a circus. And so in November 1955, Walt Disney Productions spent $600,000 on a circus tent filled with the best acts money could buy and called the thing "The Mickey Mouse Club Circus." The stands capable of holding 2,500 remained unfilled. Joe Fowler remembered: "My god, if I ever see a circus again, it'll be twice too soon…and how Walt loved it! But my god, my problems. It was the first time we learned this lesson. People came to Disneyland to see Disneyland. They weren't interested in a circus."[70]

Another company that learned this the hard way was Mattel.[71] Having learned nothing from the Mickey Mouse Club Circus debacle by dint of not

Circus World in the mid-'70s. *Courtesy of the Lake Buena Vista Historical Society.*

having been there, Mattel bought the Ringling Bros. and Barnum & Bailey Circus in January 1971. Observers scratched their heads. "Why did Mattel want to buy the circus?" they asked.

The answer came in September 1972 with the announcement of Circus World just a few miles down the road from Disney. Initial plans called merely for the construction of a permanent venue for the circus's winter residence in Florida, a tradition begun in 1927 that faded in the '60s. But by the time the project was announced, it had swollen to include a movie theater, a children's circus, European circuses and an "illusion circus." In the bold tradition of Orlando, absolutely none of these would be built.

Circus World never got too far past the initial construction of its preview center—indeed, Mattel was trying to sell it off as early as 1974. A handful of traditional carnival-style attractions sprang up around the Circus World Preview Center, which now acted as the attraction's circus arena. By the time Mattel divested itself of the Ringling Circus in 1982, Circus World had been sold to a Canadian businessman named James Monaghan. He spoke to the *Orlando Sentinel* in 1984: "Circus World has had bad management in the past. Many people I talked to had ever been because they had heard it was bad news. Everybody I talked to—bankers, people at the airport, county officials—everybody had adverse comments." The *Sentinel* continued: "The park lost about 8.8 million during 1982 and 1983 fiscal years. After the last fiscal year, [Mattel] reported losses of 19.5 million for its entertainment division whose sole entry on the books is Circus World."

Monaghan didn't have long to dwell on his acquisition. Shortly thereafter, he sold Circus World to HBJ, a book publishing company on a splashy spending spree in Orlando. HBJ shut down Circus World in 1986, reopening it as a new concept—Boardwalk and Baseball. Boardwalk and Baseball added a stadium and a late nineteenth-century atmosphere to Circus World's existing collection of rides. The idea was promising, but the park barely held on for a year before closing.

After sitting abandoned for many years, the whole area was purchased by another land developer and turned into a strip mall called Posner Park. So it goes in Florida.

10

VINELAND, DISNEY'S GHOST TOWN

They say you can't go home again, and if your home was a little place called Vineland, Florida, that's doubly true. This little nothing whistle-stop was swallowed whole by the Disney development boom; although to be fair, there was so little left of it by the mid-'60s that Disney probably didn't even know it was there.

The story of Vineland begins with the Munger Land Company. Len J. Munger and his brother Willis started Munger Land in St. Joseph, Missouri, in 1910. The brothers began snapping up cheap land in Missouri and subdividing it, and very soon they were doing the same thing in Central Florida.

The Munger parcels of land around remote Lake Ruby were christened "Orange Center." Advertisements in the newspaper said: "You can buy a ten acre farm and two choice building lots for only $250. $10 cash, $7.50 monthly; no interest, no taxes, no charges of any kind."

Yes, this was a scam. The lots were being sold through mail or telephone, but a single lot wasn't large enough to build a house on—you had to have at least two. Regardless, many people bought it, and the *Sentinel* pages through 1914 are filled with notices of transfers of property from Munger to individuals far and wide. By 1914, the *Sentinel* reported that Orange Center was home to eighteen orange groves on 140 acres,[72] and the Orange Center School had twenty-five students in 1918. But as local resident Fern Lowery said, "It was just a post office and a little store. There was never nothing there to amount to anything."[73]

Part of that reason may be because the Munger Land Company imploded into an ugly tangle of foreclosures and litigation in 1924. That same year, Orange Center rechristened itself Vineland. This rechristening involved the post office and chamber of commerce changing their names one day in July. High winds and storms had damaged huge swaths of citrus in 1920, and some local farmers were experimenting with grape growing after the example set by Dr. Phillips. Local newspaper stories extolling the virtues of the land for sale in Vineland read exactly like the promotional puff pieces they were. If all of this sounds suspiciously like a scheme to attract more landowners to Vineland, well, that's exactly what it was.

But the 1920s also saw the town's population peak at the lofty number of 120.[74] At this point, the town consisted of a single store, some orange groves, the post office, the school and a depot for the Atlantic Coast Line at the end of Eighth Avenue. In 1929, E.B. Morey—the local manager for Munger Land and presumably the motive force behind most of the sales—joined forces with M.G. Kibbe to create the "Florida Vinelands Company" and sell lots for poultry and small-scale vegetable farming. A new plat was drawn up—the promotional machine was revved up—but no sales are recorded in the *Sentinel*, indicating that the scope of their plans sank with the economy. Inland areas like Orlando simply rode the coattails of the Florida land boom, and when the twenties ceased to roar, the effects were felt quickly. Life settled into a quiet rural solitude in Vineland.

Just how rural? Let's open up the *Sentinel* on January 4, 1930, and read all about the doings down yonder in Vineland:

> **Giant Still Found West of Vineland**—*What is said to be the largest still ever found in Orange County was seized yesterday by Deputy Sheriffs J.A. Caruthers and Jim Bass at the edge of a swamp about five miles West of Vineland. It had a capacity of 600 gallons. Two men sighted near the still made their escape. The still was hot when officers arrived. About 2,500 gallons of mash and 20 gallons of whiskey were destroyed.*

If that's five miles west of Lake Ruby as the crow flies, that would put the moonshiners smack in the middle of what is today the Magic Kingdom parking lot. That swamp would be the same one that would thwart Disney planners in 1967 and necessitate the construction of the Seven Seas Lagoon. Like I said, the more you scratch at the surface of Walt Disney World, the weirder it gets.

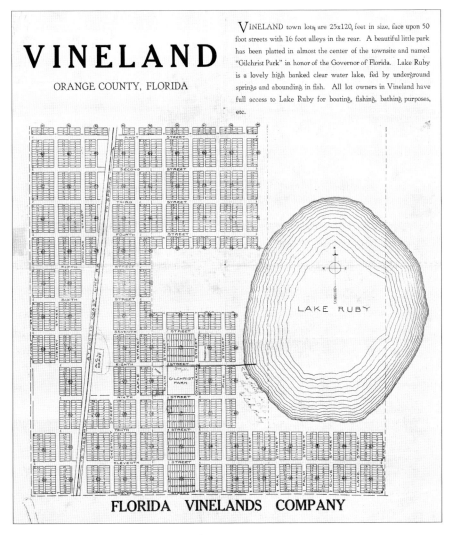

Courtesy of Orange County Regional History Center.

Vineland received its own hard surface clay road in 1932, finally connecting it to the rest of the community. This road ran from Tinker Field down through the untouched wilds skirting the edge of the Phillips groves, through Vineland and ending at the Lake Bryan Sand Mine. Some of this right of way still exists today as Apopka-Vineland Road and soon would become the site of jalopy races in the later '30s and early '40s. Besides a sawmill,[75] the remote road was considered to be a good dumping ground for trash and car bodies, a bold tradition that continues in rural areas of the Sunshine State today.

At some point in the 1940s, the Vineland post office was shuttered, with services moving up to Dr. Phillips. Residents continued to move out. The Sun Oil Company of Texas briefly investigated the area west of Vineland and Bay Lake for oil drilling possibilities, but nothing ever came of it. On April 7, 1949, Vineland was finally electrified, becoming the last section of Orlando to have power lines run.

Jock and Fern Lowery opened the gas and grocery store that would one day become Johnny's Corner following World War II, bringing much-needed options to Vineland. As Fern's daughter Susan recalled in 2010, "I came home from school one day, and Momma said, 'You'll never guess who we waited on today—Walt Disney.' We couldn't believe it. We'd see him on TV every week, and Momma was starstruck."[76] Vineland may

Photo by the author, July 2023.

have been the last part of Orlando to get electricity, but it was the first part of Orlando to get Disney.

Today, scarcely any of Vineland still exists. Motorists zip along Apopka-Vineland Road, oblivious to the fact that Vineland used to be an actual place. Much of the original Vineland street grid was wiped out by the Palm Parkway development in the '80s.

But if you drive off the main road and head east, odd pieces of Ninth, Eighth and Seventh Streets still randomly connect and dead-end at spots where roads were once meant to be. It's a sleepy, spooky time warp of a place hiding away on Disney's front doorstep. Most locals call this area "Lake Buena Vista," the name of Disney's municipality to its west. Can Vineland be forgotten if nobody remembered it in the first place?

In 2019, Unicorp National Developments announced a billion-dollar development across 350 acres on the opposite side of Lake Ruby known as "O-Town West." Featuring malls, hotels and apartment complexes, the resulting rise in property values seem poised to wipe out what little is left of the original Vineland neighborhood. In 2022, construction workers building a new Publix Supermarket on Daryl Carter Boulevard arrived on site and discovered that their new parking lot was slated to be built on the site of the Vineland Cemetery, containing exactly two graves of Civil War veterans. Owner Scott Henderson had refused to sell the twenty-five-by-twenty-five-foot plot of land containing the graves.

They went ahead and built the parking lot around it. This author could never have invented a better metaphor.

PART III

THE VACATION KINGDOM OF THE WORLD

Be fair, alright? Everyone wants Mr. Toad's Wild Ride.

–Brodie, Mallrats (1995)

11

THE FRONT GATE

When Disneyland opened in 1955, you had to pay to get in. We today may nod our heads sadly at this, but in 1955, this was news to anybody who wanted to see what Walt Disney had just spent $17 million on in a former orange grove. Disneyland was the first modern amusement zone with a gate price. Walt Disney was so adamant about this distinction that he would tell his operations managers: "You've got to control our gate."[77]

In 1955, Disneyland was operated very much on the model of traditional amusement parks, with "Disneyland Inc." acting as a landlord and leasing out space to concessionaires. The gate price reflected the fact that the built environment inside its walls was just as much an attraction as anything else. Admission was a princely $1.00; then once you got inside, you paid for each individual attraction you cared to experience—from $0.10 to $0.75 each. To put this in perspective, at this time you could buy a minute sirloin steak for dinner at Howard Johnson's for $0.95, so just admission to Disneyland had about as much buying power as a decent lunch.

There was endless harping about the cost at the time. And despite the official version of the story, which implies that Disneyland was an instant success, there was a price drop pretty quickly.

This was done by packaging a number of ride tickets with the cost of admission so that customers weren't constantly thinking about spending money while inside the park. Van Arsdale France recalled, "Ed Ettinger, head of public relations, came up with the idea of a ticket book. That way we could advertise, 'Admission and eight rides: $2.50.' Ed worried and said, 'I'll either be a goat or a hero.' He was a hero."[78] The innovation quickly became standard in the industry.

Very soon, Disneyland attractions became sorted into categories. Simple attractions and exhibits—things like the corporate-sponsored exhibits in Tomorrowland or the authentically fitted firehouse on Main Street—were "free" or at least covered by the gate admission. The lowest-cost attractions were things like the Main Street Vehicles or the Carousel, with the high end being The Jungle Cruise, the Tomorrowland rocket ride and so on. The ticket book system subsidized the smaller attractions by providing easier access to the larger ones.

This immediately had two knock-on effects. The first is that most visitors used ticket books instead of buying individual tickets, and the second is that Disney was incentivized to make any new attractions as opulent as possible to place them in this "top category" and return investment quickly. Three tiers of attractions were four by 1956 and five by 1959. This fifth category—the fabled "E" ticket—remains in the vernacular for a top-of-the-line experience to this day.

All of this shaped the way Magic Kingdom was built in 1971. The preference for ticket books on the part of the buying public meant that Disney

Amateur slide. *Author's collection.*

had to offer a full range of options on opening day, from A tickets all the way up to E tickets. This constrained the ability to build, requiring the things like a thrill ride or a copy of Pirates of the Caribbean be deferred until later. Walt Disney World president Dick Nunis later commented specifically on Pirates, saying, "To add that one attraction we would have had to eliminate five more."[79] Smaller priority attractions like the Keelboats and the Railroad languished with less detail and attention paid to their ride experience due to the need to open with five categories of attractions at once.

Disney also had to guess at what to build. Management gambled that the average visitor would skew older, which is why Magic Kingdom opened with no roller coaster but huge air-conditioned theater shows at the entrance to each land. This led to some odd circumstances, with Pirates of the Caribbean (added in 1973) and the Starjets (added in 1974) being marketed as "thrill" attractions in the interim before Space Mountain opened.

Even the assignation of ticket values was flexible: the Magic Kingdom's opening year E ticket roster was The Jungle Cruise, Tropical Serenade (Tiki Room), The Haunted Mansion, 20,000 Leagues Under the Sea, It's A Small World and The Mickey Mouse Revue. When Country Bear Jamboree and The Hall of Presidents proved to be breakout hits, they were quietly elevated to "E" ticket status in early 1972 and the Tropical Serenade and Mickey Mouse Revue demoted to their place in the "D" ticket roster.

The arrival of pay-one-price admission was slow but inexorable. Disney had been selling Magic Kingdom Club memberships to corporations since the '60s, allowing members to buy flat-price tickets known as Magic Key Coupons good for any attraction. What forced Disney's hand was the looming opening of EPCOT Center in the early '80s, a venture in which Disney had asked corporations to sink large sums of money into sponsored "pavilions," which were the main attractions.

It was never going to be easy to tell American Express that its millions had bought an attraction "worth less" than the one GM was sponsoring, so the easiest solution was that the ticket book system had to go.[80]

So what was it like to visit Magic Kingdom in the ticket book era? After paying for parking at the Main Entrance,[81] visitors would arrive via tram at the Main Entrance Complex—today known as the Transportation and Ticket Center. Here, guests could line up at ticket booths to buy their ticket books.

The first ticket in this book was good for transportation to the park via monorail or ferry boat and was torn out and surrendered at the station. The next ticket was the admission ticket, and what followed were ride

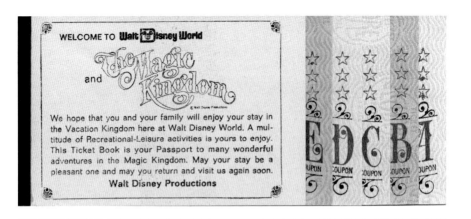

Top and middle: October 1971 Ticket Book. *Author's collection.*

Bottom: Example B Ticket from the mid-'70s. *Author's collection.*

Converted ticket booth in Adventureland, circa 1991. *Courtesy of Mike Lee.*

tickets—between 7 and 14, labelled A through E. As a rule, the books contained more high-value tickets. Of course, any of these tickets could be purchased individually, so if one wanted only to purchase admission and shop on Main Street, one could do so.

While waiting in line at Magic Kingdom, you will notice that many attractions have a place where either one line splits into two lines or two lines form into one line. This area, known as the "merge point," used to have turnstiles and a large locked metal box about four feet high where the individual ride tickets were collected. Usually, cast members stationed at this spot would have a little patter as they prepared riders to surrender their coupons, for instance:

> *Ladies and gentlemen please have your E coupons ready as you approach the Jungle Cruise....That is the E coupon, as in Extremely Excited Elephant...*

The coupons were dropped through a slot into the padlocked metal box, which was wheeled down to Cash Control every night and counted. *Yes, really.*

If a potential pirate or Tom Sawyer Island Explorer found herself without the correct ticket, each area of Magic Kingdom had a ticket booth where individual coupons could be purchased. Since Disney usually succeeded at upselling visitors on the purchase of a new ticket book under the premise that the tickets would never expire,[82] these individual ride tickets are now pretty rare.

Above: "Magic Key" Coupons good for any attraction, circa 1977. *Author's collection.*

Left: Latter-day passport ticket from 1990. *Author's collection.*

Disney seems to have been reticent to raise the price of the biggest attractions beyond the $1.00 threshold—The Jungle Cruise cost $0.75 at Disneyland in 1955 and $0.95 at Walt Disney World in 1980. That's either some serious property devaluation going on, or the "true" cost had already been simply swallowed up by the ticket book system. Still, assuming that Disney was making $0.90 per rider and that a ride like Pirates of the Caribbean can process about 2,800 riders per hour, over the course of an eight-hour operating day, that's still a huge chunk of change.

There are remnants of the ticket windows, of course, as well as pinch points where the ticket boxes once were. Stand at the exit of The Haunted Mansion, and you will hear mournful voices sing:

> *If you would like to join our jamboree / there's a simple rule that's compulsory / mortals pay a token fee / rest in peace, the haunting's free…*

…a subtle tribute to the ninety cents you once had to surrender to experience the attraction.

12

Whose Main Street USA?

Everybody wants Main Street to be their hometown. If you ride the Walt Disney World Railroad or take any one of Disney's official tours, cast members will tell you that Main Street is inspired by Walt Disney's hometown of Marceline, Missouri. Which is logical, but it isn't true.

In the last decades of his life, Walt made quite a show of speaking of Marceline and supporting the park's downtown—even sending over a Disneyland attraction and installing it in the town's public park.[83] Thanks to these very public appearances, Marceline became permanently intertwined with the Walt Disney life story and therefore with the Main Street USA myth.

Except, as can be quickly confirmed with the briefest glances at Google Street View today, Marceline looks *almost nothing* like Main Street USA. Walt was a city boy; he spent more of his youth in Chicago or Kansas City than he ever did in Marceline. The brief life experience in the bucolic small town of his youth was made ever more poignant by the fact that he was thrust back into urban life thereafter.

Now if you go out to Disneyland in California, there you will find a Main Street that is much more credible as having been inspired by small-town Missouri in the early years of the twentieth century. The buildings are smaller and less ornate, the train station looks more like a rural whistle stop and the overall effect is quite different. Surely *this* is the small Midwest town of Walt Disney's youth. Well, again, it depends on how you look at it.

Another place frequently cited as an influence is Fort Collins, Colorado, where production designer Harper Goff grew up. Goff was a designer on

May 1972. *Courtesy of the Lake Buena Vista Historical Society.*

Disneyland going way back—back when the park was an exhibit across the street from the Disney Studio in Burbank. As with Marceline, the connections beyond the autobiographical are questionable; it's not as if a train station and Victorian architecture are unique to Marceline or Fort Collins.

The reality is that the production designers on Main Street in 1955 simply cobbled together architecture from books and magazines of whatever looked right. As designer John Hench put it, there "never was a Main Street like that." And when it came time to bring Disneyland east to Florida, Main Street was moved with it.

In the late '60s, the designers at Disney were concerned that ideas and concepts represented at Disneyland be translated effectively to their new East Coast audience.[84] What they landed on for Main Street was more *Hello Dolly* than *Music Man*—a citified Eastern Seaboard town. In promotional material, they consistently cited Atlantic City as the kind of atmosphere they were hoping to evoke.

This is yet another case of printing the legend, because unlike at Disneyland, where Main Street is spun out of whole cloth, the Main Street at Walt Disney World is based specifically on Saratoga Springs, New York. We know this to be the case because Disney built perfect replicas of Saratoga landmarks on Main Street: the Train Station and the United States Hotel.

Amateur slide. *Author's collection.*

From the 1840s to the early 1900s, Saratoga Springs was the Las Vegas of its era. It had a racetrack, mineral springs and restaurants—which were sort of the equivalent of beaches and roller coasters for people of that era. Saratoga was America's first resort town, making it an appropriate touchstone as the entrance to Magic Kingdom. But why exactly did Disney settle on Saratoga?

Honestly, I'd give a lot to know. One clue may be the 1945 Warner Bros. film *Saratoga Trunk*, which was actually shot in the decaying old United States Hotel and re-created the train station with special effects. The fact that these two buildings represented in the film are those rebuilt in Florida is suggestive. Most of the core art directors who designed Magic Kingdom were previously employed in film production design in Hollywood, but I can find no direct link. Maybe somebody was just a fan?

Regardless, the Saratoga Depot, which burned in 1899, was resurrected and has welcomed vacationers to Magic Kingdom for fifty years now. The United States Hotel can be found just inside the park to the right and is currently known as the Main Street Theater. Once you know that the building was designed to be a hotel, it will be impossible to unsee it.

In a broader sense, we can see that the desire to find some link between the theme park's entryway and a real American small town is due to the historical significance of the Main Street area. After World War II, automobiles and highways threatened to destroy these traditional city centers. Disneyland opened at nearly the same time as the Southdale Center in Edina, Minnesota, the first of the massive indoor shopping malls that promised to replace urban blight.

But the Disney attractions in California and Florida demonstrated how a historic area could be green, leafy, vibrant and pedestrian friendly. People began coming home from vacations and wondering why *their* old downtown areas weren't more like Main Street USA. In time, this idea coalesced into action. The National Trust launched Main Street America in 1980, and after decades of effort, young people are finally moving out of suburbs and back into these traditional, walkable urban centers. Disney's toy city was the fake that saved a thousand real places.

But here's the question, the question that's the real crux of the issue. Why does Main Street still work? After all, in 1955, it meant something very different than it means today. In 1955, the beginning of the twentieth century was still in living memory, and indeed much of the early marketing for Disneyland focused in on this aspect, of the area being educational for young baby boomers. It was Walt Disney's virtual childhood—not really any different than the intense longing today's Gen Xers and elder millennials feel

The United States Hotel in Saratoga, New York, in 1939. *Courtesy of the New York State Archive.*

for video arcades and shopping malls. But modern visitors still respond to it; it doesn't feel like a throwback to somebody else's idealized past.

Some of that has to do with that imprecise "x factor" that architect Charles Moore called "conviction." But I think there's more going on here. No matter where you're from in the lower 48, you probably know an area in your immediate area that's a lot like Main Street. Less idealized, less well kept, but still recognizable. As Umberto Eco put it, Main Street belongs "to a fantastic past that we can grasp with our imagination."

Or as John Hench said to Beth Dunlop, "Painters do this. You can't paint sunflowers without referencing Van Gogh. He expressed a whole truth.… In much the same way, we own Main Street, because we expressed the archetypal truth about Main Streets everywhere."[85] In other words, every visit to The Magic Kingdom starts by sending you home.

Today, both Marceline, Missouri, and Fort Collins, Colorado, boast of being the true inspiration for Main Street. Fort Collins has a massive mural of Harper Goff downtown; Marceline visitors can visit the Walt Disney Hometown Museum. Many small towns have installed electrical facsimiles of gas lights, post clocks and festoon lights in imitation of the Disney Main Street. It can be hard to remember that these features were inspired by Disney's original fake and not the other way around. Main Street has become everyone's hometown through pure force of will.

And as for Saratoga Springs? This author has walked Saratoga's main street, and the overall effect definitely suggests that at least somebody visited the real deal before embarking on the design of Main Street in Florida. Perhaps after some local reads this book, that fascinating connection will finally be recognized and celebrated.

13

Disney World Gets "Citrusized"

Florida Citrus and Mickey Mouse.
Motherhood and apple pie pale in comparison.
—*Dorothy Chapman, laying it on a bit thick,*
Orlando Sentinel, *December 28, 1970*

Citrus was king in Florida. My great-aunt drove through Florida in the 1920s when the price of gas was a nickel. She spoke often of driving through the scented winter orange groves that seemed to stretch from coast to coast. And while citrus remains a huge part of the state's identity, the bad old days of the citrus ranches and packinghouses have safely joined *The Yearling* in Florida's mythological past.

And if there's anything that Disney will soak up like a ShamWow cloth absorbing off-brand cola, it's the mythological past. This is the story of Walt Disney World and Florida citrus, the bad marriage that created a cult icon.

In 1967, Disney was shopping for sponsorship suitors for Walt Disney World. The Florida Citrus Commission was interested. The Citrus Commission—FCC—is a state-run board funded by taxes paid on citrus products. This means that any money the commission was going to spend is tax money, and especially in states like Florida, this is a big deal. If the Citrus Commission wanted to tango with Disney, it was going to have to step lightly, but first it needed government permission. The Florida legislature gave permission to the Citrus Commission to negotiate with Disney in January 1968. Early plans called for an informational exhibit in Tomorrowland,[86] along with an orange juice bar at the Preview Center.

Vintage postcard © Disney. *Author's collection.*

But by October, plans had changed, and by "unanimous choice," the FCC was now sponsoring the East Coast version of the Enchanted Tiki Room. Perhaps due to the sudden shift from exhibiting orange juice to exhibiting space-age singing birds, the public was repeatedly assured that the agency's money was being spent on promotion.

Edward A. Taylor, executive director of the Citrus Commission, declared that "Disney World will be 'citrusized' from start to finish." The details of the final agreement included a display wall promoting citrus products, an exit area show with tiki gods praising the benefits of orange juice, a snack stand that featured citrus recipes developed by the Citrus Commission and a real citrus grove to be maintained by Disney. FCC parted with $3 million, and the contracts were signed on October 22, 1969.

But that was not all. In December 1970, Taylor hinted that Disney had designed a "very secret" character for use by the Citrus Commission. This, of course, was the Florida Orange Bird, which was unveiled with Florida Citrus spokeswoman Anita Bryant in March 1971 at the Florida Department of Citrus headquarters. Bill Bentry, of the *Tampa Tribune*, noted that "Orange Bird is a 'he' determined from the way he cuddled Miss Bryant during a picture taking session." Yeesh.

On opening day, most of this advertising muscle materialized. In a pre-show, Clyde and Claude toucan make their appearance from behind a magic waterfall perched on "Citrakua," a god who appeared to be crushing oranges in a huge bowl with a paddle. Oranges festooned the Magic Fountain inside the theater show. Sadly, the "Tiki God post show" never appeared.

But definitely on hand was the ubiquitous Orange Bird, which perched in a swing above the Sunshine Tree Terrace snack bar at the attraction's exit. This static figure swung back and forth and had "orange thoughts" projected above his head. In the early days, the snack bar dispensed creations from the Florida Citrus Growers labs, such as frozen orange juice bars and "Citrus Salad Gel" garnished with tangerine and grapefruit wedges.

October 6 was dubbed "Citrus Day at Walt Disney World." Ceremonies included Governor Reubin Askew opening the pavilion with "the squeezing of an orange."[87] As the dedication ceremonies proceeded, workmen were just cleaning up the site of the installation of a citrus grove bordering the attraction's pre-show area.[88]

Florida Citrus spokeswoman Anita Bryant sang a few songs, including two from the forthcoming Orange Bird record, and then guests proceeded into the pre-show, where Governor Askew was apparently roasted by Clyde and Claude toucan.[89]

Throughout the early 1970s, much excitement can be found in Florida newspapers for the Sunshine Tree Terrace, which regularly rolled out experimental citrus products from the Florida Citrus Growers laboratory in

A 1970 press release photo of the Orange Bird. *Courtesy of the Orlando Public Library.*

Lake Alfred. The hits included the "Citrus Salad Gel" (ten thousand sales a week), an "isotonic citrus thirst quencher," a "Citrus Slush" (four thousand sales a day) and, um, an "O.J. Hot Sipper" (never to be spoken of again).

Meanwhile, Orange Bird proved to be a hit. The Disney children's records sold briskly, the bird appeared alongside Anita Bryant in nationally televised commercials and Florida Citrus Growers even sponsored an "Orange Bird Sweepstakes" in 1974.

Plates, trays, spoons, jewelry and stuffed animals all were produced. Citrus stands across the state jumped on the bandwagon with Orange Bird displays and standees, often homemade. A girls' softball team in Clermont, Florida—home of the Citrus

Tower—dubbed themselves the Orange Birds. The Florida Department of Citrus received fan mail for the Orange Bird, including a card from one deaf little girl in Chattanooga who sent him a valentine on which she wrote, "I love you Orange Bird."[90]

In other words, Disney and Florida Citrus had a genuine hit on their hands. Children performed Orange Bird school plays. College students decorated with Orange Bird balloons. Department of Citrus events invariably included multiple inflatable orange birds at the entryway. The Plant City Strawberry Festival tried out a copycat mascot, Mr. Strawberry.

And yet, in the background, the relationship between Disney and the Florida Citrus Commission was gradually souring. The first public cracks appeared thanks to a 1980 educational film, *Food and Fun*, paid for by the commission to the tune of $350,000. The film is an inoffensive twelve-minute production in which Orange Bird must eat a balanced diet and exercise in order to be fit enough to fly south for the winter. The film includes a bizarre scene in which the Orange Bird pours himself a tall glass of OJ. Despite the plug, the film wasn't "citrusized" enough for the commission.

"I am bitterly disappointed by what I saw....I saw more milk and cheese than oranges," blustered Citrus Commissioner Walter Woolfolk.[91] Another commissioner, David Hamrick, opined: "The message was so damn subtle that I missed the point." The commission required a revision in which the phrase "orange juice" was used twice. At the same time, citrus industry columnist Bob Bobroff reported that forthcoming negotiations with Disney for a renewal of the contract for the Sunshine Pavilion might become tense.

And yet the renewal was signed, extending the contract five years through 1986. The Citrus Commission asked that the Sunshine Tree logo be placed more prominently on the entrance sign, that the entrance or pre-show be modified to directly mention Florida citrus and that displays of citrus products (finally) be added to the exit corridor. Additionally, Florida Citrus Growers asked for a second location to sell citrus products, which was duly constructed—the Enchanted Grove in Fantasyland was built in 1982 (now the Cheshire Café).

For the next few years, the Orange Bird returned to his yearly duties of appearing in the Citrus Parade and officiating at Florida Citrus Growers events, even if his signature "split-open orange mobile" was junked in 1982. But the 1980s were a rough decade for "King Citrus," with freezes and rampant citrus canker decimating millions of acres of product. The USDA prohibited the shipping of Florida citrus products to other citrus-producing states, such as California. Texas sued Florida to prevent shipments of Florida grapefruit into the state. Profits plunged. In the midst of all of this, Disney came back for more money.

This page: A 1972 cookbook pamphlet with Disney and Orange Bird cross-promotion. *Author's collection.*

In the 1987 renewal negotiations, the new Michael Eisner regime at Disney proposed increasing the yearly fee to $285,000. Florida Citrus Growers responded by requesting improvements to the Tiki Room show. Disney drew up a proposal to flatten out the tiered waiting area to the attraction to install benches and talking tiki gods.[92] The cost of this renovation was pegged at $600,000[93]—all of which, naturally, FCC was on the hook to pay.

The commission balked. It proposed sponsoring The Diamond Horseshoe Revue instead. Talks stalled. And on July 29, 1987, the Citrus Commission voted to let the sponsorship end. "We can't afford Disney," said Chairman Bill Becker.[94]

It's hard to blame them. Even in the heady early '70s, some citrus growers were heard to comment that the Enchanted Tiki Room really had nothing to do with citrus.

The commission held that the attraction's appearance and sound quality had deteriorated, a trend that would only continue through the Eisner years. Without the motivating sponsorship, the Orange Bird passed into history and was forgotten.

...*and yet!*

Walt Disney World has rarely emphasized the historic character of its attractions to tourists. Still, there were passionate fans out there from the start. One of these was Mike Lee, who grew up down the road from Disney World in the early '70s. By the late '80s, Lee had begun tinkering with a fan zine devoted to old (for then) Disney World, and in the late '90s this tinkering went online in the form of the seminal website Widen Your World. In the year 2000, Mike published the first written history of the Orange Bird, and young readers like me were smitten.

There were fewer resources like the one you hold in your hands right now, and so fewer people used fewer sources to get their Disney World history. Anybody who cared at all about early Disney World got all of their information from Mike. And so for those of us geeky enough to care, the Orange Bird became a secret handshake of sorts, a quick way to identify those who looked for more than the official history of the property in Florida. From there, his fame grew.

And in due time, it came to pass that some extremely dedicated fans inside the company managed to engineer the return of the Orange Bird on April 17, 2012. The character was featured on the sign of the Sunshine Tree Terrace, his theme song was rerecorded and a raft of limited time merchandise was sold. Most importantly, an original Orange Bird figure was located in California and brought back to Florida. Since the original Sunshine Tree itself was disassembled during a renovation in 2000, he now stood on a crate of oranges at the rear of the snack stand.

```
                          TROPICAL SERENADE
                   Proposed Pre-Show for Walt Disney World
                                 3/13/87

SCHEME 1:  see attached treatment for show detail

       elements                      waterfall over kiosk
                                      animated orange tree with birds in it
                                      5 tiki gods around room

                                      new floor layout with benches to enhance
                                      the patio atmosphere

                                      new interior dressings

                                      new spiels by birds

SCHEME 2:  -- reduced show with 2 tiki gods on either side of kiosk, animated
           tree

Chief show difference:  Limited "Magical element." Birds carry on shorter
pre-show dialog with guests, the two tikis and animated tree come to life.
There are fewer objects for guests to observe during their waiting time in the
pre-show.

       elements                      waterfall over kiosk
                                      animated orange tree with birds in it
                                      2 tiki gods on either side of kiosk

                                      new floor layout with benches to enhance
                                      the patio atmosphere

                                      new interior dressings

                                      new spiels by birds

SCHEME 3:  -- reduced show with 1 tiki god

Chief show difference:  "Magical element" is removed.  Birds carry on shorter
pre-show dialog with guests, leaving less "entertainment" time in the area.
The orange tree does not magically grow fruit, nor does it talk.  There are
fewer objects for guests to observe during their waiting time in the pre-show.

       elements                      waterfall over kiosk
                                      orange tree with birds in it
                                      1 tiki god

                                      new floor layout with benches to enhance
                                      the patio atmosphere

                                      new interior dressings

                                      new spiels by birds
```

```
          WALT DISNEY WORLD CO.

                  MEMORANDUM


TO    Steve Bills                  DATE    October 7, 1987

FROM  Al Shacklett  al   EXT 7278  SUBJECT   Tropical Serenade Show


   Based on a recent discussion with Chuck Luthin, we agreed that the
   best evaluation approach for the proposed new Tropical Serenade show
   is to compare its cost per unit of capacity with other proposed new
   attractions.  The following table provides this comparison:
```

ATTRACTION	INITIAL INVESTMENT	AFTER-TAX NPC	HOURLY CAPACITY	COST PER UNIT OF HOURLY CAPACITY
Mickey Mouse Revue	$8 M	$8.7M	+1,569	$5,540
Star Tours	$46 M	$11.2M	2,300	$4,870
Splash Mountain	$43 M	$20.9M	2,000	$10,450
Fantasy Gardens	$8-11 M	$19.9-22.1M	2,500	$7,974-8,858
Tropical Serenade	$5 M	$3.6M	+335	$10,728

```
   In comparing these proposals, it is also important to consider the
   expected utilization of the added capacity for each of the attraction
   proposals.  We are confident that the first three listed attractions
   (Mickey Mouse Revue, Star Tours, and Splash Mountain) would be fully
   utilized on the Design Attendance Day.  However, for Fantasy Gardens
   and Tropical Serenade, the additional capacity may not be utilized as
   effectively as the first three attractions due to lack of sufficient
   guest demand.  If we use attraction utilization on the Design Day as
   our performance measure, guest demand for Tropical Serenade must
   increase by at least 30% for the above cost per capacity figure for
   Tropical Serenade to remain valid.  If guest demand were to increase
   by 20%, the comparative cost per unit of "effective" hourly capacity
   would actually be $18,000.

   Based on this comparison, we feel that priority should be given to
   Mickey Mouse Revue, Star Tours, and Splash Mountain above the proposed
   new Tropical Serenade show.

   AS/bc

   cc: Chuck Luthin
       Rob Mitchell
       Bill Sullivan
       Donna Templin
       Bob Ziegler
```

This page: Internal memorandum explaining proposed changes to the Tropical Serenade for the Florida Citrus Growers' potential 1987 contract renegotiation. The second page paints a bleak portrait of the attraction's prospects to increase capacity. *Author's collection.*

To populate Walt Disney World's entertainment lineup, Disney went on a nationwide talent hunt. In Hawaii, it found the musical duo of Gary Stratton and Bob Christopher, performing at the Schooner steakhouse on Waikiki. Brought back to Orlando, Gary and Bob's smooth folk crooning and audience heckling was an immediate sensation. They were a headlining act at Grad Nite and the opening of the Lake Buena Vista Shopping Village, where they presided over a lounge inexplicably known as "The Chummery." The two were even swept up in a dispute Disney was having with Orlando over improvements to State Road 535. Gary and Bob recorded a song, "Can You Arrive Alive on 535," which included lyrics such as: "Even Bonnie and Clyde back in 1925 would have taken I-4 instead of 535."

Disney sent out free copies to local radio stations, where it was a momentary local sensation. Orlando fixed the road. The song has since apparently vanished.

And that trick that occurred in the early '70s repeated itself. Even if nobody really knew what the little guy was doing there, they liked him just the same. What was first intended to be a limited-time event has just continued rolling along, as shirts, hats, pins and plush toys have just not stopped being made. Orange Bird has, against odds, become the unofficial mascot of both local Annual Passholders and the EPCOT Flower and Garden Festival. To the surprise of everyone, the Orange Bird received a golden statue for Disney World's fiftieth anniversary. It seems once you put this little citrus bird in front of the public, they just can't stay away.

But the Orange Bird isn't just cute—he is a *local*. Time was, citrus was king in Florida. Time was…never to return. The Orange Bird represents this, bridging past and present far more nimbly than Mickey Mouse ever could. He lingers on, ensuring that Disney World remains "citrusized" from start…to finish.

14

Bear Tracks Looking Back at Me

Country Bear Jamboree has always been just a little weird.

Up until 1971, absolutely nobody except Walt Disney would have said that the best thing to do with bears is have them play musical instruments. That idea is already strange enough, but then take it further and say that not only will bears be playing instruments, but they will also be starring in a musical sendup of *Hee Haw*… it's such a bizarrely specific set of ideas and references, seemingly snatched out of thin air. One reaches to imagine scenarios where white lab coat–wearing scientists were feeding information into one of those massive 1970s supercomputers in an effort to predict the next Hanna-Barbera cartoon.

So how did we get here? Why did Disney build Country Bear Jamboree? Surprisingly, the whole thing started with skiing.

Following its initial success, it was not at all clear if the special accomplishment of Disneyland was destined to spill out into multiple entertainment facilities nationwide. After all, successful restaurateurs open multiple restaurants and successful directors make multiple movies; there was not yet any indication that there was to be only one Disneyland.

Walt fielded proposals from around the world; Europe, Japan and Australia were all clamoring for their own Disneylands. New York wanted him to buy Ellis Island.[95] St. Louis and Kansas City wanted him to redevelop their downtowns into tourist attractions. Walt seems to have at least momentarily taken some of these ideas seriously.

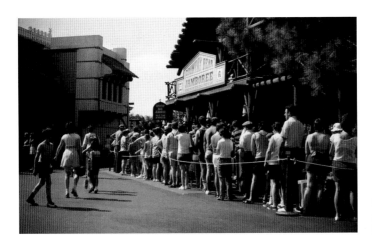

*Courtesy
of Michael
Crawford.*

To put this in perspective, motion pictures represented 77 percent of the Walt Disney Company's revenues in 1954 but only 46 percent in 1966—yet overall revenues were up 800 percent.[96] Disney invested in a massive indoor recreation center in Denver, the Celebrity Sports Center, and made films for World's Fairs in Italy, Brussels and Montreal. But the idea that seems to have gotten the most active engagement with Walt was at Mineral King Valley in California.

The Mineral King area had been under active consideration by the U.S. Forest Service for a ski resort since the end of World War II.[97] Mineral King had been the site of an uneventful gold rush in the nineteenth century, meaning it had a crude road constructed into its interior and thus was considered to no longer exist in its "natural" state.[98] And that road into Mineral King passed right through Sequoia National Park, meaning that two very different governmental agencies were going to have to work together if the Forest Service wanted to develop Mineral King.

Independent of all of this, Disney had hired Buzz Price to research locations for a ski resort in the early '60s. Price zeroed in on Mineral King, and suddenly the Forest Service had the golden opportunity of bringing in Walt Disney as a partner at Mineral King.

Walt wasted no time. Just as he was doing in Florida at exactly the same time, Disney authorized Bob Hicks to begin snapping up available land in Mineral King.[99] And just as he would do in Florida, Walt's project represented a dazzlingly massive proposal. Disney was promising skiing for twenty thousand, ten restaurants, twenty ski lifts, multiple hotels, a ski school and a Swiss village.[100] The Forest Service saw dollar signs all around and approved Disney's plans.

The issue was the proposed road into Mineral King. The local government of Three Rivers, California—population two thousand—flatly rejected the tab for the $25 million highway, and neither Disney nor the Forest Service was going to foot the bill. The money was going to have to come from the state or federal level. After some political wrangling from Walt, the State of California approved construction of the highway into Mineral King. But even before the road reached this point, it seemed doomed. The Park Service adamantly opposed it, passing as it did near some old-growth redwoods within Sequoia National Park.

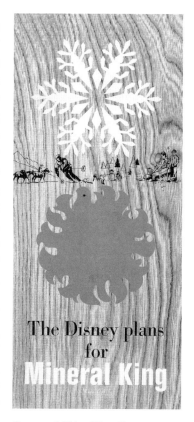

And then there was the matter of energy; were we going to be building a power plant in Mineral King? The idea of building a station inside the valley seemed sacrilege. But there was no good spot *outside* of the valley, and the idea of transporting thousands of cars plus power, water and waste across a tiny ribbon of road built in

Courtesy of Ted at DisneyDocs.net.

the nineteenth century seemed impractical. Disney, for its part, took the same position it did in California and Florida: the infrastructure is your problem, the leisure area is our problem.

Lurking in the background through all of this was the Sierra Club. Through the '60s, the club had grown from an enclave of old-school sportsmen types to one more explicitly concerned with environmental conservation. The Sierras and several other groups around the country, opposed on principle to any development in Mineral King, began a lengthy and embarrassingly public campaign. A public hearing on expanding the Sequoia Wilderness Area became a venue to turn public attention to Mineral King. Both sides brought their arguments to the podium, hijacking a meeting that wasn't about Mineral King at all. The ploy worked, and the public became increasingly swayed by the apparent inevitable intrusion into "virgin land."

To be fair, this is more than knee-jerk NIMBYism.[101] Disneyland was surrounded by what Disney admitted were "honky-tonks," and given everything you've learned about what happened to Orlando in this book, it's easy to understand fears of overdevelopment. Disney means money, money means people and those things will absolutely change a place irreversibly.

What was worse, Walt Disney died in 1966. At the end of his life, Walt Disney was at the height of his power to "sell" ideas, and without his reassuring presence to cut through opposition as it had in Florida, this was becoming an uphill climb for Walt Disney Productions.

With all of this drama as a mere backdrop, Walt went to his top designer, Marc Davis, with an idea. Marc remembered: "Walt was looking for things that would make people stay overnight…not just have them go out and ski but before it got dark have these attractions that would keep them."

WED Enterprises mechanical engineer Wathel Rogers elaborated: "Walt said, what we're going to do is have a bear band and have them perform two or three programs of entertainment. We'll say that the bears had come down out of the sequoias and we trained them to be entertainers!"[102] Marc dutifully got to work, knowing his boss would want to see the widest array of options possible. He drew marching band bears, cowboy bears and torch singer bears. These early concept explorations were one of the last things Walt Disney looked at before he checked himself into St. Joseph's Hospital and died.

With Walt suddenly gone, the question everywhere at Disney was how to proceed. Now, this was the point where Roy Disney—who had for so long been the cautious counterpoint to his brother—could have easily sounded a retreat from costly and risky ventures like Mineral King. But he did not.[103] Roy gathered up all of Walt's creative executives in a projection room one week after Walt's death and announced: "We're going to finish this park, and we're going to do it the way Walt wanted it. Don't you ever forget it."[104]

So the "bear band" was integrated into Magic Kingdom at Walt Disney World. The show entered production in early 1968, with story director Al Bertino choosing songs, developing gags and continuity and Marc Davis designing characters. The duo homed in on country music as the most likely choice—what else would critters from out in the holler sing? George Bruns, a Disney composer best known for "The Ballad of Davy Crockett" and "Yo Ho Yo Ho A Pirate's Life for Me," came aboard. Bruns brought an unhinged go-for-broke edge to the songs that remains infectious and impossible to duplicate today.

The final show, a kind of head-on collision between the Enchanted Tiki Room and *Hee Haw*, was a technical triumph of its day and a monster hit. It was so successful that Disney quietly upgraded it from a D ticket to an E

Marc Davis (*left*) and Al Bertino (*right*) go over an early storyboard for Country Bear Jamboree. *Courtesy of the Orlando Public Library.*

ticket in January 1972, swapping the D ticket rating over to the Tiki Room (one wonders if Florida Citrus Growers objected).

The road into Mineral King was never built, and the area was ultimately absorbed into Sequoia National Park. Disney tried again, this time on public land near Lake Tahoe, but Independence Lake also died on the vine. Country Bear Jamboree would go on to entrance a young man from Utah named Nolan Bushnell, who founded Atari and, later, Chuck E. Cheese. The deluge of Chuck E. Cheese imitators in the early '80s would give robotic animal stage shows a bad name, but Country Bear Jamboree remains an artful and entertaining show; the bears really do seem to live. Far too many walk past today without giving the venerable old show a thought, but there's a reason why the bears have played on for five decades now.

15

Take Aim at History

Y ou probably walked right past the Frontierland Shooting Arcade. It's easy to miss; it doesn't look like much from the outside, and it's situated just inside Frontierland behind some trees. But step through the entrance, past the knotty wood logs holding up the porch, and you will be reliving hundreds of years of amusement park history. *Hold on*, you may ask; *why is there a shooting gallery here anyway?* Well, there's a story there…

Shooting galleries as amusement enterprises date back as far as the production of standardized firearms, but they seem to have really begun to take off in the middle of the nineteenth century. "Game hunting" in the nineteenth century was often an excuse to go out into the countryside with a pack of friends and get as drunk as possible, and the association between shooting and conviviality lingers in a lot of the early history of shooting gallery games. These were often built attached to "Exchanges" (read: bars), alongside bowling alleys and pool halls. J.E. Brophy advertised in the *Daily National Democrat* of Marysville, California, in 1860:

> *The undersigned, having re-established and completely re-fitted the well known SHOOTING GALLERY near the corner of D and Third Streets, is now ready to receive the public. All the arrangements are perfect, and every thing will be conducted in the approved style.…THE BAR attached to the Gallery is superbly arranged, and the LIQUORS of the choices kinds.*[105]

One imagines that one of those elements was more important than the others. If you are reading this and were born in the twentieth century, you may have grown up going to locations where video games and pinball existed in the same location as pool tables and bowling alleys; as you can see, these associations go far back.

Once these informal clusters of diversion began to congregate in particular parts of town—perhaps near beaches, restaurants or hotels—we have the foundation of the amusement park. That's how Coney Island began, with its infamous clusters of bars and pool halls, along Surf Avenue.

And it is this particular era of the shooting gallery that explains how we have our gallery in Frontierland. In 1955, Disneyland opened with a shooting gallery on Main Street USA. The Penny Arcade attraction on Main Street was a knowing re-creation of the state-of-the-art of amusement in 1890, with mutoscopes, "love testers," orchestrion devices, twinkling electric lights and mechanical games. At the back of it was a shooting gallery. Patrons lined up and shot at moving ducks and rabbits with Winchester Model 62A pump-action air rifles.

Nearby in the Davy Crockett Arcade, a planned exhibition of miniatures called "Disneylandia" never panned out, and Disney, in a big hurry, put up some costumes and props from Davy Crockett on display. Designer Sam McKim modified a few Seeburg "Shoot the Bear" and "Raccoon Hunt" machines to appear to be situated in a forest glade. "Old Betsy" rifles were anchored to artificial tree stumps, and the whole scene was surrounded by overflowing displays of Southwest and Mexican handicrafts intended to recall the atmosphere of the Alamo.[106]

Both Main Street and Frontierland galleries were owned and operated by a local outfit called MacGlashan Enterprises, which supplied the guns, made the shot and even repainted the galleries nightly to avoid unsightly shot marks.

The MacGlashan ranges must have been a success, because an expanded Shooting Gallery opened in Frontierland in 1957, then another in Adventureland in 1962. Disneyland's shooting gallery empire was established.

In the mid-'60s, Walt Disney began to buy out contracts of the licensees who ran Disneyland to bring the entire operation of the park under the control of Walt Disney Productions. In February 1969, Disney announced it was acquiring MacGlashan for an unspecified cash amount. By this time, MacGlashan was operating galleries in Ohio's Cedar Point, Six Flags Over Texas and soon Opryland USA in Nashville. It's fascinating to think of Disney getting residuals from Opryland.

Courtesy of the Lake Buena Vista Historical Society.

And so the Magic Kingdom Frontierland Shooting Gallery opened in 1971 pretty much under the control of Disney, and throughout the 1970s, Imagineering and MacGlashan cooperated closely. MacGlashan introduced a light gun range product they called the MacGlashan "Lazer Gun" and began to convert shooting galleries across the country. One place that had this installation at least into the '90s was Cedar Point, making for some strange six degrees of separation.

In time, it made sense to convert the Disneyland and Magic Kingdom shooting ranges to light gun technology. Imagineer Pat Burke recalled that he worked with Sam McKim on a new "ghost town" light gun shooting gallery for Disneyland and Magic Kingdom.[107] Pat recalls doing this work in 1976 or 1977; it's entirely possible, but the galleries at Disneyland and Walt Disney World were not converted until 1985. By that time, Tokyo Disneyland had already been open for two years with its Westernland light gun range. All three of these attractions exist today pretty much untouched from their mid-'80s state, a pure and wonderful slice of vintage Disney design.

And you know, the story *could* stop there. But if we just stay focused on shooting galleries in amusement parks we are missing a bigger story, a story that connects to your life at times when you are not on vacation in Florida or California. And to get there we're going to have to take a side trip to Japan.

Over in the Land of the Rising Sun, Hiroshi Yamauchi was leading his family business in some strange directions throughout the 1970s. The company that began as a playing card manufacturer was branching out into taxis, love hotels and, well, bowling alleys. That most midcentury of pastimes had been a craze in Japan, and it turns out there were a lot of bowling lanes in Japan that weren't being used. Yamauchi had a plan to turn them back into profit centers.

The name of Hiroshi Yamauchi's company, in case you don't already know, was Nintendo.

So in 1973, Nintendo introduced the Laser Clay Shooting System, a high-tech showpiece that could be fitted into however many bowling lanes operators wanted to renovate. This was a *fancy* experience, with projected clays being cast into a painted backdrop. The rifles, which could be rented or purchased, were heavy and convincing mock firearms and could be cracked open above the stock to "reload."[108] According to author David Sheff, these locations became "the hip spot for an evening's entertainment."[109]

All of this expertise put Nintendo in a unique position to manufacture toy light guns at cost, which is how it ended up being contracted by Magnavox

Amateur slide. *Author's collection.*

to manufacture a toy light gun for the pioneering Odyssey video game machine. As far as I can tell, this was Nintendo's first contact with home video gaming devices.

But the true turning point for Nintendo came later. Nintendo was testing the waters in arcades hoping to pave the way for the release of a home video game system. It noticed that one game in particular, an electronic shooting gallery called *Duck Hunt*, was a hit with Americans.[110] This game was unremarkable in Japan, but Americans loved shooting at the colorful ducks. A second game mode had players shooting clay skeets, an intentional callback to the Laser Clay location–based games.

And so when Nintendo's Famicom was released in the United States as the Nintendo Entertainment System, Nintendo made sure to pack in *Duck Hunt* and a toy gun with every last system sold. As you may have heard, Nintendo's ventures outside of Japan have turned out well. It's fascinating to think that the worldwide success of Nintendo and the rebirth of video games are tied so intimately to a shooting gallery.

So step up to a gun in Frontierland, take a few shots and linger awhile. Enjoy the clever scenery and details designed by Sam McKim and Pat Burke. Try to shoot the livery stable to reveal the bucking bronco. When you do so, you are participating in a tradition that stretches from the Wild West through to the creation of amusement parks and on to your home PlayStation.

16

Dreams of Glowing Flowers

Riders today wait in long lines for a trip through Peter Pan's Flight in Fantasyland. Peter Pan's Flight is unique among its peers at Magic Kingdom for having hardly changed at all in the fifty years it has been open, and part of how you can tell this to be true is the blacklight look of the ride. The lurid glow of the interior scenery is somewhere between charming and dated, but what it *is* is historic!

The earliest self-illuminating process to be common in commercial applications was radium. The phosphorescent qualities of radium had long been known to scientists, but the first company to begin extracting radioactive materials and applying them to consumer products was the United States Radium Company in Orange, New Jersey.

Alexander Strobl, one of U.S. Radium's key employees, left its employ to set up his own company—Stroblite—in 1924. A Stroblite catalogue on file at the Smithsonian lists products for sale in the categories of Adhesives, Candles, Lamps, Lighting, Medical, Paint and Trade Shows.[111] By the 1930s, Strobl had moved on to ultraviolet lighting effects and was marketing a wide range of paints, lamps and supplies for producing strange glowing effects. These illusions were widely used onstage, for illuminated landscapes, instant costume changes and novelty dance numbers.

All of these splashy applications of the effect date to the mid-'30s, which seems to have been ultraviolet light's big "coming-out" party. At the New York 1939 World's Fair, General Electric demonstrated the effect in its *House of Magic* show, in which brilliantly colored columns seemed to appear around the audience when the lights were extinguished. Across the country at the Golden Gate International Exposition in San Francisco, blacklight effects highlighted statuary and frescoes to startling effect.[112]

Interestingly, UV paint and amusement parks had at this juncture not yet come together. The earliest dark ride was developed by Leon Cassidy in 1928 and was an entirely blackout affair, intended as a sort of thrilling Tunnel of Love. Chicago's Harry Travers copied Cassidy's idea and added a succession of startling effects to the experience such as kicking mules, lightning strikes and oncoming trains. In order to remain competitive, Cassidy's Pretzel Amusement Company began to sell black box "stunts" to operators, such as illuminated leaping skulls and snapping alligators. These were lit with incandescent bulbs, usually amber or red, hidden inside the boxes. The figures in the boxes were almost always either cardboard or papier-mâché.

It seems that the company that really took the use of UV light in dark rides mainstream was Disney. The original 1950s versions of Peter Pan's Flight, Mr. Toad's Wild Ride, Snow White's Adventures and Alice in Wonderland were glowing phantasmagorias of uncanny sights. UV lights were used to present the Satellite View of America, a huge mural view of the United States from space viewed from a moving walkway. The climax of the Mine Train ride in Frontierland was the Rainbow Caverns, a display of glowing, dyed water fountains set to ethereal music. The effect was so novel Disney sold glowing rocks and UV posters next door in a shop called the Mineral Hall. Competitors took notice and, as they did for many such innovations made mainstream at Disneyland, followed their lead.

Maybe the most noteworthy of these competitors was Bill Tracy, an independent dark ride designer based out of New Jersey. Tracy's company got contracts to update the old Pretzel and Travers dark ride installations across the country and did so with his signature lurid glowing colors and bizarre, gory characters. As the '60s turned psychedelic, the associations between UV light and hippie culture were embraced by Tracy, who added serpents coiled around glowing peace signs to his attractions. I'm sure upright middle Americans were horrified.

But as the UV effect went mainstream—in dark rides, funhouses, miniature golf courses and discotheques—Disney began to back away from its use. The 1971 fleet of Magic Kingdom dark rides proved to be one of the final times its use was widespread. As part of the 1983 rebuild of Fantasyland at Disneyland, designer Tony Baxter began to consciously intersperse scenes lit in incandescence into the blacklight attractions. The connotations of the look were no longer favorable or cutting-edge. It's amusing to think of an

Above: Mr. Toad's Wild Ride interior. *Courtesy of How Bowers and the Lake Buena Vista Historical Society.*

Left: Snow White's Adventures ride operator giving the "Hold Sign." *Courtesy of Mike Lee.*

effect that every American recognizes on sight was, less than one hundred years ago, a novelty startling enough to be used on Broadway.

Today, Peter Pan's Flight is the last traditional dark ride still standing at Magic Kingdom. Snow White's Scary Adventures was considerably toned down in 1994 and then removed entirely in 2012. Mr. Toad's Wild Ride, the beloved psychedelic head trip designed by Rolly Crump, was replaced by The Many Adventures of Winnie-the-Pooh in 1998. This means that Magic Kingdom's Peter Pan's Flight is the very last Disney dark ride in the United States to still exist in a form close to its original installation. With its tournament tent façade, simple effects and cheerful Day-Glo interior, it is the nearest you can get to zipping back to 1955 and witnessing the attractions that revolutionized the industry.

So, yes, its garish orange flowers may speak to the hippie era and its recorded music and sound effects sound like they were recorded at the bottom of a well and you can totally tell that the interior of the volcano is crumpled-up aluminum foil. But I hope that Peter Pan's Flight stays just as it is for a long time to come, the last neon holdout in our modern world.

17

Movies from the Future!

Disney is, at its core, a movie company. Walt Disney moved out of Kansas City to Hollywood in the hopes of directing motion pictures, all of his early employees did likewise and all of the people who designed Disneyland and Walt Disney World worked first and foremost in the motion picture industry. Many of Walt's attraction designers began as animators. When Walt Disney was planning to build Disneyland, he went to his architect friend Welton Beckett for advice. Beckett told Walt, "No one can design Disneyland for you. You have to do it by yourself."[113] Walt turned around and raided the art department of 20th Century Fox, which was imploding at that time. The design language of theme parks that they created is innately linked with the language of film.

This is still evident in a number of ways around the park, including the fact that Main Street USA has a cinema and a penny arcade but not necessarily a grocery store. The much-touted forced perspective used around the park is really just a movie studio backlot trick reproduced inside of a public space. But one of the ways that this is most evident is in the fashion that Disneyland and Magic Kingdom presented innovative and futuristic movie experiences.

First, some context. Hollywood of the Golden Age was a vertical monopoly; movie studios controlled the production and distribution of films because they owned the theaters that the films were shown in. After the war, a number of events shook the Hollywood film industry to such an extent that it felt the need to regroup and try a new approach. The first of these was a decision handed down by the United States Supreme Court that this vertical monopoly must end; another, more fundamental threat was the rise of television as a major force in American households.

So, just like today, movies got bigger and more spectacular. Wide screen and stereophonic sound came roaring back as new saviors of the newly independent exhibition industry. Color on screen became much more frequent instead of being reserved for extremely special-case films as it had been in the 1940s. Theaters even experimented with 3D, giveaways, midnight screenings and other such gimmicks.

In 1952, stage producer Mike Todd presented *This Is Cinerama* on Broadway, a system using three interlocked projectors and seven speakers to create an immersive spectacle. The opening roller-coaster ride had audiences screaming for real. In 1953, 20th Century Fox developed Cinemascope, a special method of squeezing and then "unfolding" an image, allowing widescreen images in regular motion picture venues without the need for multiple projectors. As *Business Screen Magazine* put it, "Bigger and wider screens are the unmistakable trend of movie presentation."

Disney produced Cinemascope films such as *Toot, Whistle Plunk and Boom, Lady and the Tramp* and *20,000 Leagues Under the Sea*. Impressed by the visual spectacle, Walt began thinking of the possibilities of an even wider screen. There's nothing wider than a screen so wide it wraps around to a full circle, and so Walt Disney stopped his friend Ub Iwerks in the studio hallway one day in 1955 and suggested he look into the idea.[114] Ub—who had known Walt since 1919—recognized this as the assignment it was and threw himself into the work.

The trouble is that no camera in the world can shoot in a complete circle. The additional trouble is that due to the fact that motion picture lenses are curved, two cameras placed side by side will eventually capture the same object inside the frame at the same time. The solution arrived at was to place a six-inch gap between each screen in the theater. The second problem was, if your camera is shooting in all directions, then where is the camera crew?

Ub mounted his ring of eleven 16mm cameras to the roof of a Nash Rambler and drove around the western United States. Stops included Wilshire Boulevard, the LA Freeway, the Grand Canyon and Las Vegas. American Motors sponsored the exhibit. In a clear dig at Cinerama, Disney called its process Cir-CAR-ama.

Once the film was shot and edited on eleven different reels of film, exhibiting it was an entirely different matter. It was obviously impractical to have eleven projectionists running the show, and then of course there was

Avenue between the USSR (*left*) and United States (*right*) pavilions at the 1958 Brussels World's Fair. Vintage postcard. *Author's collection.*

the problem that if one of the projectors got even slightly out of sync the entire illusion would be ruined.

With the Disney studio entirely overextended during the construction effort of Disneyland, the Urban Engineering Company of Hollywood was awarded the contract to find a way to achieve synchronous projection. It outfitted each projector with an endless looping reel of film, similar to a Super-8 audio cassette, and attached each to a Selsyn motor that was locked in sync to the United States' 60-cycle power supply. The show could be started and stopped with a button, and a projectionist was only necessary to replace burned-out bulbs and broken film reels.[115]

All of which is to say, Circarama was an impressive technical feat in 1955 and one knocked together by the Disney studio in less than six months. Audiences stood in the middle of a room and looked up into a ring of screens hung eight feet above the floor. The *New York Times* called the show "the ultimate in audience participation." The highlight of the film was a high-speed chase down Wilshire Boulevard that nearly caused many visitors to fall over. And so, just a year and half later, in January 1957,[116] Walt Disney and John Hench were being spoken to by a representative of a think tank that had been appointed to a unique task: to determine how to represent America at the 1958 Brussels World's Fair.

The Brussels World's Fair was the first major, officially sanctioned expo to be held since 1939 and was billed as the "first Atomic fair." Earlier in the 1950s, the Eisenhower administration had secured emergency funding from Congress to participate in exhibitions and cultural events of this kind. Eisenhower viewed the public image of the United States to be essential in combating the expansionist Soviet Union, and both the State Department and CIA were plowing significant money into this world's fair in particular.

The fair opened only months after the USSR had launched Sputnik, and the Russian pavilion was directly across the road from the American one.[117] As usual, the Russian pavilion emphasized the country's technological and military might; the Americans decided to go in a different direction.

The American pavilion instead emphasized the official, sanctified version of American culture of white families in suburban homes with picket fences. This fair did much to fix this image of atomic age America in the mind of both America and the world, and the hit of the fair was the Walt Disney film *The USA in Circarama*. It is a testament to how immediately Disneyland was recognized as an all-American creation that one of its hit attractions was brought into Europe as an ambassador of culture.

The USA in Circarama ended up being sponsored by Ford to the tune of $200,000; the U.S. government chipped in another $400,000. Disney spent a year filming the show, with stops in Ford's River Rouge automobile plant as well as views of New England fall foliage, Times Square, oil drilling in Oklahoma, a wheat harvest in Montana, the Grand Canyon and, of course, a modern shopping mall and supermarket. The crew traveled in a Lincoln Premier and a Ford station wagon.[118] Live narrators presented shows in English, French and Flemish. The film created such demand that the theater routinely had a queue outside of several hours. Most visitors, including more than a few Russians, wept at the ending as "America the Beautiful" played.[119]

All of this had several knock-on effects. The most obvious was that other circular films followed. Fiat wanted a Circarama tour of Italy for the Turin 1961 Exposition; Disney produced the film. Ub Iwerks made a significant improvement to the Circarama system. This time, the motion picture cameras were not turned outward in a ring, but inward, where they filmed a reflection of the surrounding scenery in nine mirrors. There were no blind spots possible.[120]

In 1967, the nine-camera system made another leap, from 16mm to 35mm. As the conceit of mounting the camera to a moving car had been abandoned back in Turin in 1961, the circular process received a new name: Circle-Vision 360. The larger 35mm image meant larger screens and a larger

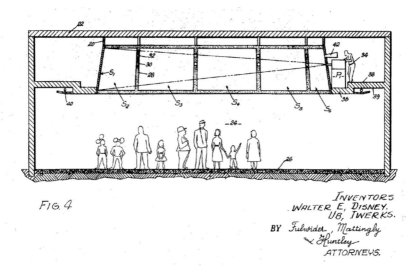

Ub Iwerks's patent for the Circarama film format. *Courtesy of the Lake Buena Vista Historical Society.*

theater were required; new metal railings allowing visitors to lean as they watched the film were added. All of these changes premiered at Expo '67 in Montreal; the Disney film was presented by the Telephone Association of Canada and called *Canada '67*.[121]

The second knock-on effect was that Walt learned very quickly that his studio could benefit in surprising ways from involvement in world's fairs. Ford had no interest in retaining any ownership of *The USA in Circarama*, clearing Disney to bring the film back to Disneyland as *America the Beautiful* in 1960. The theater itself was dismantled by the United States Information Agency and toured Europe showing the Disney film for nine years. Walt ended up coming home with a new Disneyland attraction basically for free.[122]

This arrangement is the very same one Walt Disney entered into for the pavilions at the 1964 New York World's Fair. Brussels in 1958 had been such a success that New York secretary of state Robert Moses decided to launch yet another world's fair.[123] Companies, expecting the success of 1939 and 1958 to repeat itself, signed on to sponsor the 1964 World's Fair en masse. Almost everybody lost their shirt. Just about the only person who didn't was Walt Disney, who allowed Ford, General Electric, PepsiCo. and Robert Moses himself to fund the development of the attractions, which he carried back to Disneyland. World's fairs allowed Disney to outsource research and development to massive corporations with almost no financial risk.

Circle-Vision theater under construction at Magic Kingdom, mid-1971. *Courtesy of the Orlando Public Library.*

By far the most significant of these was the General Electric Carousel of Progress. Walt Disney Productions had been attempting to develop dimensional animation since the late '50s, but the studio simply didn't have the resources necessary to get the technology operable. General Electric, the Google of its day, had millions to spend. The terms of Disney's contract at the 1964 fair meant GE could fund the development of this technology and Disney could walk away with all of the patents.

Without GE's deep pockets funding the Carousel of Progress, Disney would never have been able to create Great Moments with Mr. Lincoln, It's a Small World, Pirates of the Caribbean, The Haunted Mansion or Country Bear Jamboree. Pirates of the Caribbean and The Haunted Mansion were the additions to Disneyland that pushed that park over the ten-million-visitors-a-year line and, arguably, saved the Disney Studio following Walt's death. In this sense, we can draw a direct line from *The USA in Circarama* to the opening of Walt Disney World.

With a presentation that historically important, Disney of course kept making Circle-Vision films. A new 35mm version of *America the Beautiful* debuted at Disneyland's "New Tomorrowland" in 1967. That same film presentation opened at Walt Disney World in 1971. Disney produced three Circle-Vision films for EPCOT Center in 1982: an updated version of *Canada '67* called *O Canada!*, a new 360 film *Wonders of China* and an artful half-Circle-Vision film called *Impressions de France*. The opening of Disneyland Paris brought *Le Visionarium*, a clever combination of a circular film with in-theater animatronics and effects. This show was significantly changed and brought back to Walt Disney World as *The Timekeeper*.

But the tech-savvy '80s and '90s made these theater-in-the-round experiences look dated, and people then as now didn't like standing for the whole movie. One by one, all of Disney's Circle-Vision theaters in California, Tokyo Disneyland, Disneyland Paris and Magic Kingdom closed. The Circle-Vision theater at Magic Kingdom today hosts The Monsters Inc. Laugh Floor, having been downgraded from nine screens to three. There are finally seats, which may be why it has not yet closed.

Which means that Epcot World Showcase is the last place on earth you can take in one of these circular films. Just as in 1955, audiences mostly enjoy the scenes where the camera moves quickly and stand patiently through the rest.

But these films changed the Walt Disney Company in very real ways, ways that even this author was ignorant of before she began researching this subject. Today we take screens for granted; nobody would even think twice about the technical challenges of creating a continuous circle of images of 1955. It's fascinating to think that something most tourists see as hilariously antiquated was once considered enough of a technological breakthrough to be funded by the U.S. government and held up as a signifier of American culture in the wake of the atom bomb and the Sputnik satellite.

And if that isn't hidden history—history so hidden that even the Walt Disney Company has forgotten it—I don't know what is.

18

A Chapter about Nothing

Most writing about Magic Kingdom begins at the railroad. The Walt Disney World Railroad represents Walt Disney's love of trains, which is the "Disney version" of the story. Because I like to be different, this chapter is going to end with the railroad. And I'm not going to rehash the old stories about the Chicago Rail Fair or the Carrollwood Pacific. Instead, I'd like to draw your attention to nothing.

About halfway through the trip around the Walt Disney World Railroad, the train passes through a long stretch with absolutely nothing of interest to look at. There are trees, the rail line and a lake off to the left. To the right, you can get some unflattering glimpses of the "back side of Fantasyland."

This section of the ride has always been an excuse for the train narrator to fill some time. In the early days, the narration tried to present this area as a look at "the untouched Florida wilderness." This is why there are mechanical rattlesnakes and alligators here. Later versions have tried to pass this off as the "outskirts of Fantasyland." Both are somewhat true without being remotely inspiring. Who knew that the outskirts of Fantasyland involved so much algae?

One of the most interesting things about the original Walt Disney World project area is Bill Martin's choice to present the landscape as a version of the existing Florida landscape but dramatized. Brush has been cut back and replaced by rolling green lawns. Oak trees have been transplanted from across the property, where they perch alongside picturesque lagoons. Stands of cypress have been strategically left in place.

This page: Magic Kingdom ephemera from the 1970s: (*above left*) March 1972 Guidebook, the first ever issued for the park; (*above right*) another guidebook from early 1977; and (*left*) parking ticket from 1973. *Author's collection.*

Upon learning from research that visitors to Florida wanted to see white sand beaches and palm trees, Disney built its own ringing the shores of the Seven Seas Lagoon. These can be expediently viewed via monorail on your way to and from the park. The landscape is native, but better, more dramatic and more dreamlike than Florida ever looked. And it is absolutely designed, curated and presented to you as an impossible but credible reality.

So about that nothing. Yes, there isn't much to see, but look again. That waterway off to the left, more often than not clogged with algae, was put there by General Potter, and it connects Bay Lake to Reedy Creek.

Off to the right, the unflattering view of the back side of Fantasyland is a reminder that the train is actually traveling at the true original ground level. Magic Kingdom is built on a building on top of this original ground level but actually raked forward, allowing the train to pass over the entrance but behind the rear. Main Street is built at a slight slope, making it look longer from the entrance and shorter at the exit. No other Disney park plays these games with elevation, and it's all done on top of a massive buried tunnel complex. Even a lot of the vegetation along this back stretch was cleared away and replanted by Disney for maximum pictorial value.

In short, there's nothing to look at back there, *but almost everything you see was put there by Disney*, and that's the wonder of it. That's what made Walt Disney World such a special accomplishment in 1971—not the castle, not the monorails or the dancing mice or hamburger machines or even The Haunted Mansion. It was a totally built environment so persuasive you forget you're looking at one. All of the flywheels that keep the machinery humming are tucked away below somewhere, allowing you to ride a train pulled by a one-hundred-year-old engine across a fake hill of green grass put there by an art director and look at a shimmering but totally credible manufactured lake.

All of that effort is invisible. You see nothing.

PART IV

•———————•

EPCOT, E.P.C.O.T.
AND ALL THE OTHER EPCOTS

U p to now, your author has attempted to tell the story of Walt Disney World in basically chronological order—from vacant swamp to populated clockwork wonderland. But getting to the next step, EPCOT Center and everything that happened to Walt Disney Productions afterward, is complex and cannot be laid out so easily.

This is thanks to Walt Disney, who seemed to know he was dying, but rather than plan for this inevitability just piled obligation on top of obligation on his company in the last few years of his life. This avalanche of obligations ultimately overwhelmed and buried his corporate heirs, and in their place a new company arose from the ashes.

The second half of this book is about this process, about how a family-run studio with a few hundred employees was reborn and positioned for world conquest. By necessity, the character of the second half of this book is going to be a bit different, but it's necessary to take this ride and understand how Walt Disney Productions eventually came to be that cultural leviathan we know and fear by one name: "Disney."

19

WALT AND URBAN PLANNING

Walt Disney hated an old challenge. When *Snow White and the Seven Dwarfs* was reissued in 1944 and proved to be a big success, Roy Disney thought his brother Walt would be pleased. But instead, Walt said: "So you're in the secondhand business now."[124] Not "we're" in the secondhand business—"you" are. That story says a lot about Walt Disney.

So after Disneyland opened and became a huge success, Walt began casting about for a new muse. He began to think about solving real-world problems. If baby boomers had midlife crises and bought expensive cars, Walt Disney went to Germany and began buying mass transit. Gondola systems, modern trains, monorails—all would find their way to Disneyland.[125]

But in a sense, none of this was really new for him. Walt Disney's earliest experiment with building a functional utopia came in 1938. The old Disney Studios on Hyperion Avenue in Los Angeles had outlived their usefulness. At a time when most movie studios were slapdash utilitarian things put up where space allowed, Walt Disney conceived of his new animation studio as an orderly machine created by one designer. This was born of practicality— the immediate concern after *Snow White* was quickly converting Walt Disney Productions to produce as many as three animated features at once.

Walt's studio was physically organized in a top-down structure. Ideas flowed out from his top corner office in the animation building following an orderly downward spiral. Below Walt's offices were story men, writers and gag men on down to animators and in-betweeners. Then there was a tunnel connecting the Animation building to Ink & Paint, where the production process continued.

Walt's first utopia, the suburban-style Disney Studio in Burbank. *Library of Congress.*

Aesthetically, the new Disney studio was just as unique. Parking lots were replaced with suburban lawns, white curbs and spreading trees. Instead of concrete bunkers, the buildings were modernist cubes in California salmon and green. Just about the only thing Walt didn't provide his staff with was housing, and he strongly considered it. The new Disney plant in Burbank was neat, stylish and modern, and employees just hated it.

This reaction shocked Walt. Joe Rosenberg, a banker at Bank of America, ominously warned Walt that if he made the new studio too nice, "you will cause discontent!"[126] Whereas previously animators had worked together in good spirit, with Walt's office at the old Hyperion studio no better or worse than any other, now the Disney brothers were hidden away behind secretaries. There was an exclusive clubhouse and a secretive executive lunchroom. The new studio drew a line under those who were favored and those who were not.

And indeed, Walt did cause discontent. In order to finance the studio, the brothers had to take out another loan with Bank of America, a loan that was supposed to be paid off with the success of *Pinocchio* and *Fantasia*. When both of those films underperformed, Walt had to do a drastic workforce reduction.

Fewer people were doing more work for the same money. This eventually boiled over into a bitter animation strike, an event Walt never tried to understand and deeply resented. He expected his employees to understand the $2 million campus as Walt's generous gift to them. Those who didn't get with the "Walt Program" often found themselves frozen out. The strike shattered his utopia.

The itch for a utopian workplace society reasserted itself in the last few years of Walt's life as he launched a series of projects consciously intended to secure his legacy. The resort at Mineral King was intended to be a utopia of recreation in balance with the natural environment. In order to secure an ongoing supply of talent for his studio, Walt wanted to set up a "City of the Arts" in California, a college campus where every art form would be taught and embraced.

And most famously, he bought those forty-seven thousand acres in Orlando and wanted to build a city of the future—E.P.C.O.T. The existence of a Disneyland-style theme park on the same property was intended as a mere formality. Walt toured shopping centers and new communities around the country, gathering material for his Florida project. He had Herb Ryman create some bold art to help "sell" the idea. He even secretly spoke to General Electric about the possibility of purchasing Walt Disney Productions to help realize the project.[127]

In October 1966, Walt Disney sat down for his last filmed appearance, enthusiastically pitching the E.P.C.O.T. city to a lone audience of one camera. Brilliantly underplaying Marty Sklar's script, Walt proposed a massive suburban city with an enclosed downtown, buried highways and train lines and a radiating spoke of suburbs extending out from the center, all serviced by mass transit solutions already proven at Disneyland.

Even as Walt was enthusing, "Speaking for myself and the entire Disney organization, we're ready to go right now!" he was so sick he had to be administered oxygen to keep filming. It's a brilliant performance, one that has continued to move audiences sixty years after it was recorded. Anybody at a loss to understand how Walt Disney time and again managed to rally huge investments on crazy schemes need only watch this film. It is the only Walt Disney sales pitch preserved for posterity, a master at his craft in the last days of his life. But it is also important to remember that the E.P.C.O.T. presented in the film was only a starting point, a big goal to place off on the horizon to get everyone moving in the same direction.

Walt died a few weeks later. Marty Sklar recalled, "It was a great idea but only Walt could have made it work."[128]

Everyone at Disney seemed to sense this. Amazingly, Walt was the sole point of contact between his creative staff and the rest of the studio. Sklar

The Herb Ryman concept painting for E.P.C.O.T. that would haunt the Disney organization for thirty years. *Promotional slide from the author's collection.*

again: "When Walt died, Roy had been in the WED building only once, to my knowledge, and Card [Walker] and Donn [Tatum] not at all."[129] The rest of the company had to be brought up to speed, and fast. Marvin Davis, the master planner of Walt Disney World, went up to Roy's office to present the existing plans for E.P.C.O.T. He showed Walt's brother the buried highway, the monorail lines, the suburbs laid out like the spokes of a wheel.

At the conclusion of his presentation, Roy looked Marvin right in the eye and said simply, "Marvin…Walt's dead."

20

LAKE BUENA VISTA

The City of the Future

Since December 1971 and the death of Roy Disney, the Disney company had been run by a coalition of people loosely organized by the board of directors. These were Donn Tatum, Card Walker and Ron Miller. Card Walker had been a Walt Disney acolyte since the days of *Snow White and the Seven Dwarfs*, and Donn Tatum was a former television executive. Ron Miller was Walt Disney's son-in-law. These three had a heck of a job on their hands.

The big problem with Walt Disney's E.P.C.O.T. plan is that nobody ever worked out exactly how Disney was supposed to manage a city of the future. Walt seemed to believe it would all be worked out once the project got rolling, the way it always had.

But people are messy and unpredictable, and messy and unpredictable are entirely opposed to the entire ethos of E.P.C.O.T. Having citizens would mean that those citizens would have to be extended voting rights, voting rights that could easily fly in the face of Disney's entire reason for buying forty-three square miles in Florida: control.

For a real-world example of this, look no further than New York City's Roosevelt Island, which installed a trash HVAC system modeled on the one at Disney World.[130] The HVAC system has been a costly disaster for five decades now. This is because in real life, people do things like try to cram entire beds down HVAC systems, making maintaining the entire system a costly affair. Multiply small things like that times one thousand, and you have a picture of why getting anyone to actually live inside E.P.C.O.T. was going to be sticky.

Very early sales book from the Lake Buena Vista Preview Center. *Author's collection.*

For a while, Disney considered having only employees living on property or perhaps having temporary rotating housing. One participant in these meetings recalled: "You can ask one question: 'Where shall we put the cemetery?' That put a lot of things in perspective."[131] But eventually, they focused in on a solution that was already working in Florida just up the road, a solution that they were spending an awful lot of time hanging out in. This was Bay Hill, Florida, a golf community partially owned by Arnold Palmer.

If having full-time residents was an impossibility, then a vacation community inside Walt Disney World seemed to be much more in line with the company's goals. And so in December 1971, Disney rolled out the red carpet for Lake Buena Vista, its first serious attempt and first real failure to make E.P.C.O.T. a reality.

The Walt Disney World Preview Center became the headquarters for the Lake Buena Vista Land Company, a venture headed up by Bob Foster. Disney was building clusters of condominium-style buildings, in one or two bedrooms with a bonus sleeping loft. Emile Kuri, who had set-dressed everything from *Mary Poppins* to The Haunted Mansion, was on call as the house designer. Disney pitched horse riding trails, a golf clubhouse, a shopping center and— one day—a peoplemover and commercial facilities. The condos leased to corporations and individuals for between $5,000 and $7,000 a year. This was about the median annual salary of Americans in 1972.

And here's the thing: they actually did this. The golf clubhouse and eighteen-hole course were in place by 1974, as were about eighty condominiums. A group of energy-efficient Fairway Villas was being constructed alongside the golf course. And in early 1975, Disney unveiled the "Lake Buena Vista Shopping Village," a cluster of about forty shops and restaurants huddled around the "Village Lagoon."

This was patterned closely on trendy shopping complexes in Southern California,[132] but the sophistication was no joke. The Gourmet Pantry sold steaks and fresh produce, the Vintage Cellar had a fine selection of wines and you could stop by the Flower Garden on your way back to your $7,000-a-year villa via a rented sailboat. From the outside, the project seemed a success.

But Lake Buena Vista was just another side hustle for Disney. Walt Disney World had proved a runaway success, but the executive team was cautious and frightened. Demand for hotel rooms around Disney World was exploding, but CEO Card Walker obstinately refused to build more hotels to capitalize on this. He said, "Disney is not in the hotel business. It's in the parks business."[133] Those condos and villas housed not residents but tourists.

Left: An atmosphere of sophistication prevailed at the Lake Buena Vista Shopping Village, seen here in 1978. *Amateur slide, author's collection.*

Right: Shopping and dining brochure from 1978. *Author's collection.*

Those who stayed at the villas loved them, but Disney never advertised them heavily. You just had to know.

Meanwhile, the Shopping Village was beloved, but mostly by Orlando locals. The Wine Cellar was the best stocked store around and offered a membership club where locals could come in and fill a box monthly. The Village Lounge began booking top-name jazz acts, which drew crowds of music students from as far away as Tallahassee; the lounge had to institute a door charge. It was an enticing destination for those in the area, but tourists never quite found their way to the Village. Changing the name to the Walt Disney World Village and adding a massive steamboat restaurant in 1977 didn't seem to help.

By then, some of the more innovative aspects of the Lake Buena Vista project began to die on the vine. Plans for an elaborate peoplemover lay dormant. Unlike the versions at the parks, this was envisioned as a "horizontal elevator" where a push of a button would summon an individual electric pod to scoot you off to a chosen destination. The peoplemover was to

This page: Views of the Shopping Village in the '70s. *Courtesy of the Lake Buena Vista Historical Society.*

> In 1973, Disney opened a new branch of the company, Community Transportation Services, intending to market its mass transit solutions to cities around the country. Although posterity remembers the 1970s for gas-guzzling cars and gas shortages, there was actually a boom of interest in mass transit solutions during the Nixon administration. Disney leadership figured that since they were the only people in the country who had been operating a proven monorail system for fifteen years, municipalities would come knocking.
>
> Municipalities did not come knocking. The only nibble of interest Disney received was from of all places the Houston Intercontinental Airport, where it replaced an existing—faulty—peoplemover system. Disney's "secret" peoplemover still carries passengers through its air-conditioned, carpeted underground twilight zone to this day.

connect to a regional multimodal station, with monorails running to Magic Kingdom. But as it always seems to, mass transit in Central Florida stalled out and seemed to kill the peoplemover with it.

If all of this seems eerily familiar, it's because we've already looked at a similar example in this very book: Florida Center. I'm convinced that the failure of Florida Center very much scared Disney off its ambitious plans. If Florida Center, located basically where Florida's Turnpike and I-4 crossed, was too remote to attract residents, what chance did Disney have?

And this left Disney in a real bind. It had, after all, promised Florida a city of the future. Florida had granted Disney special privileges—even the ability to build an airport—for the purpose. The specter of Walt and his "unfinished business" nagged at the mind of the executive team. Card Walker, especially, felt he and the company owed it to Walt to deliver something called EPCOT. This phantom boss would become the driving factor behind Walt Disney Productions for the remainder of the decade, the ghost of the boss with his feared raised eyebrow.

21

HURRY UP AND WAIT

People don't want thirteen million guests a year tromping through,
looking in their living room.
—Jack Lindquist

As the 1970s rolled on, it became increasingly clear that Disney had no idea what EPCOT was going to be. At a press conference in 1972, Walker exclaimed: "We really don't know what EPCOT is or how to get ahold of it. But everything we learn as we go along will go into the planning of EPCOT!"[134]

Florida politicians and journalists, for their part, never relented in raising the question. And so, in 1975, Card Walker announced with great fanfare that the opening of Space Mountain represented the completion of "Phase One" of Walt Disney World (debatable) and that the company would be moving forward on EPCOT. Which was great...except...it still had no concrete plan.

What the company *did* know is it wanted to build a World Showcase on the banks of the Seven Seas Lagoon, pretty much on top of where the Magic Kingdom parking lot is now. This was envisioned as a huge cluster of two semicircular two-story buildings, with each nation provided equal frontage space around a central courtyard and each "wedge" extending behind that.[135] The overall effect looked something like if Space Mountain were a doughnut instead of a macaron.

Model of the standalone World Showcase attraction. Promotional photo © Disney. *Author's collection.*

At a point where EPCOT was still an amorphous series of blobs based around such ideas as "communications" and "computers," World Showcase seems to have firmed up as a concept amazingly quickly. Already in place was the idea to staff each pavilion with representatives from home countries, whom Disney expected to house in an "International Village," which, in concept renderings, looks like some kind of themed shopping mall.[136] Disney even opened an office in Washington, D.C., to solicit nations and lured C. Langhorne Washburn away from the Ford administration to run it.

Ominously, Disney expected each nation to fund and operate its own pavilions, with Disney selling its design services to each client and acting like landlords for each slice of the pie. But as Jack Lindquist pointed out to Edward Prizer, "Governments just don't move as fast as we do."[137] This bizarre arrangement was a recurring theme under Card Walker, and it's the deal Disney insisted on for Tokyo Disneyland. Because of this, Disney missed out on all of the revenues from the most profitable theme park in the world, instead having to make do with a measly stipend of $40 million a year.[138]

EPCOT was at that point not nearly as conceptually advanced as World Showcase. Card Walker—in reality writer Marty Sklar—lays out the case in the 1975 Annual Report:

We believe that in order to attain Walt Disney's goals for EPCOT we must avoid building a huge, traditional "brick and mortar" community which might possibly become obsolete, in EPCOT terms, as soon as it is completed. EPCOT's purpose, therefore, will be to respond to the needs of people by providing a Disney-designed and Disney-managed forum where creative men and women of science, industry, universities, government and the arts can develop, demonstrate and communicate prototype concepts and new technologies, which can help mankind to achieve better ways of living.

In short, Disney was proposing to form an *administration company* that would manage a series of industrial centers for research, which it dubbed "Satellites." All of this research would then be presented to the paying public at an "EPCOT Future World Theme Center" in which Circle-Vision films, models and ride-through attractions would inform the public on subjects being researched at the "Satellites."

If all of this sounds bizarrely and needlessly complicated, well, that's what potential sponsors thought too. Keeping one research-focused company headed in one direction is tough enough; coordinating enough of them to make any one of these "EPCOT Satellites" worthwhile was going to be a fool's errand. As Sklar later said, "It all had the 'sound' of EPCOT, but without the 'community' part."[139]

The end of Walker's 1975 letter really demonstrates just how out of its depth this entertainment company was:

We envision the EPCOT Future World Theme Center as a long-range, non-profit project, whose pavilions and exhibits will be financed by interested governmental agencies, corporations and foundations. We will contribute whatever land is necessary and make the Theme Center available to Walt Disney World guests free of charge.

By 1976, it appears that somebody at Disney had done some sobering cost analysis on all of this. World Showcase was speeding along at a good clip, whereas the Future World Theme Center was mainly the subject of admiring glances and polite applause. It was increasingly clear that building two separate facilities and expecting giant corporations to play nice was not going to produce a viable product, so in 1976, Marty Sklar and John Hench famously pushed together the two models and created EPCOT Center in the "figure 8" we know it as today.[140] This was at the suggestion of John DeCuir Jr., who was the master planner for both projects.[141]

Walt Disney World Showcase news

VOL. 1, NO. 3 • WINTER 1975 WASHINGTON, D.C. 166 K Street, N.W., Suite 708, Washington, D.C. 20006

World Showcase Effort Covers the Globe

Disney team visits Russia, Poland

Two top Disney executives recently visited the U.S.S.R. and Poland as part of the continuing World Showcase communications and research effort.

The team included Dick Nunis, Executive Vice-President of Operations for Disneyland and Walt Disney World, and John Hench, Executive Vice-President at WED Enterprises, the Disney "Imagineers" responsible for creating World Showcase pavilions.

Dick Nunis (l.), and John Hench board the supersonic Concorde jet enroute to Russia and Poland to continue World Showcase effort.

In Russia, the busy schedule included top-level sessions with the Soviet Chamber of Trade and Industry, the Russian counterpart to the U.S. Chamber of Commerce. Included in the talks was Sergey Nikitin, Chairman of the Administration for Foreign Tourism. The meetings were arranged by Soviet Ambassador Anatoliy F. Dobrynin.

Additional sessions were held with Viktor Boichenko, Chairman of INTOURIST, the state tourism organization and a key agency within the U.S.S.R. INTOURIST is the government agency that assists foreign visitors within the U.S.S.R. and Soviet tourists headed abroad.

According to the latest Europa Yearbook, tourism is a developing industry within the Soviet systems. In 1972, for example, more than 2.2 million foreigners visited the Soviet Union — including 66 thousand Americans.

Following the Russian visit, the Nunis and Hench Showcase team traveled to Poland for a continuation of talks with that country.

Meetings with Dr. Wlodzimierz Wisniewski, President of the Polish Chamber of Commerce, and Jerzy Zelislawski were part of the visit. A luncheon with other tourism and foreign trade officials was also included.

The trip allowed the team to present the preliminary concept for a Polish pavilion at World Showcase.

The concept is based on a traditional Polish folk-hero, Twardowski, who has been animated to act as host for visitors to the pavilion. Authentic Polish foods, music, and merchandise will be part of the total experience.

Wisniewski and Zelislawski visited Walt Disney World earlier this year for a thorough briefing on the workings of the Vacation Kingdom and plans for World Showcase.

Hummel joins German industries in World Showcase

Goebel Art (GMBH), manufacturers and designers of the world reknown Hummel ceramic figurines, has signed a letter of intent to participate in a German pavilion at World Showcase. The letter of intent, signed by Herr Wilhelm Goebel, indicates that a complete line of Hummel ware will be available at the pavilion in a specific area.

continued

Employee newsletter covering the World Showcase effort, January 1976. *Author's collection.*

The pieces fell into place rapidly after that. General Motors signed on as a sponsor in 1978; John Hench asked Marc Davis to return from retirement to design concepts for the World of Motion ride. With one major backer in place, enough corporate sponsors began to drip in to populate the rest of the Future World Theme Center area.

Harper Goff returned to WED to work on the EPCOT concept and suggested breaking each World Showcase pavilion out of its concrete bunker and allowing each to meander pictorially along the lagoon.[142] The twin crescents of the old World Showcase instead migrated into Future World, where they became CommuniCore.

By 1979, EPCOT Center had evolved into the shape it took on opening day. Unlike Walt's city, it was something Disney knew how to build, and unlike the EPCOT Satellites, corporate sponsors could control the message of each attraction inside Future World.

EPCOT Center, for all of its faults, was more or less consistent with Walt Disney's brand of futurism: that technological progress would all by itself lead us to a better world. This attitude, by design, tallied very well with the goals of the corporate sponsors of the individual pavilion and seemed to bolster their own claims of benevolence—even if, to cite two examples that really happened, they were marginalizing the possibilities of alternative energy sources or mocking competitors to the combustion engine. Those were details subordinate to the overall gestalt.

In September 1982, journalist Edward Prizer boarded the final monorail to the "preview" of EPCOT Center. The monorail passed above the park just as it does now; the passengers unloaded at the EPCOT Station and gathered on white benches to watch a television presentation. Prizer struck up a conversation with the couple sharing his monorail car.

> *"What happened to the city of the future?"*
> *"You remember that?"*
> *"Yes," she said with a chuckle, "I was going to move up here after they got it all done."*
> *"It was only an idea. A starting concept. It wouldn't have been practical to have people making their home in a showplace like this. Don't you really think this is better?"*

The lady wasn't so sure, but I'm with Prizer. Disney chose the best viable option.

E.P.C.O.T. was originally an acronym, because that's the only thing it could be when it was a bold, if sketchily defined, idea—a concept that needed explanation. In the '80s, it became EPCOT Center because that's the only thing it could be in the 1980s environment of American corporate culture. Today it's Epcot—comfortably lowercase Epcot. *Everybody* knows about Epcot—it requires no introduction.

22

BUILDING THE TWENTY-FIRST CENTURY

"You might say that each and every one of us is a crew member here on…
spaceship earth!" [applause] "When will we say that?"
"Anytime. Dinner…literally any time."
—Wet Hot American Summer

On October 1, 1979, Card Walker woke up in his cottage in Bay Hill. It was a bright and balmy day in the mid-eighties, with a gentle breeze. That Monday morning, he headed out to a field of dirt two miles south of the Contemporary Resort and stuck a shovel in the ground. Construction on EPCOT had officially begun. The day had been long coming and probably felt like a culmination of a lifetime of effort for him. But little did Card know that his troubles with EPCOT had only just started.

To begin with, the budget had ballooned alarmingly. Initially budgeting for $300 million, Disney had expected corporate sponsorships to contribute some $350 million. By the time the project was made official, Disney's share had become $500 million, and by groundbreaking it was at $800 million. In all that time, the participation agreements with the corporate sponsors did not keep pace with the project's inflation, staying right at $350 million. By the time everything was said and done, Disney had spent $1.2 billion on EPCOT Center. It had expected to fund about half of the project but ended up funding four-fifths of it.

EPCOT Center Groundbreaking. Promotional photo © Disney. *Author's collection.*

Disney had developed nine attractions for Future World. Two of the nine—Life and Health and The Seas—had failed to attract sponsors and were placed on hold. Two more, Kodak's Imagination and General Electric's Horizons, had fallen behind schedule and been cut from opening day. Spaceship Earth was nonnegotiable as the icon of the park, but Dick Nunis felt they could open the park on the basis of Universe of Energy, World of Motion, Communicore and The Land. One could have added, they didn't have much choice.

Construction work was handled, at the suggestion of Ford Motor Company's Lee Iacocca, by Tishman Construction.[143] Tishman had overseen construction of the World Trade Center in New York and basically invented the practice of construction management. Unlike with J.B. Allen in 1969, Disney really did have the best in the industry on this new job.

Disney would need the expertise. Leadership had chosen a site roughly in the center of property; thus the name "EPCOT Center."[144] The entire site was checkered with flooded underground caverns, caverns that ballooned the size of the World Showcase lagoon. For caverns that could not be avoided, construction crews pumped out water and swamp sludge and filled the crevices with sand. As had become tradition during the construction of a Disney park in Florida, a huge sinkhole was discovered on-site. World of Motion was relocated, and the sinkhole became part of World Showcase lagoon. The sinkhole still lurks below the water in front of the Odyssey Restaurant.[145]

From the start, Disney knew it wanted a big, impressive United States of America show to anchor the park, but ideas were slow to evolve. Marc Davis tackled the question by conceptualizing a ride-through attraction based on a populist panorama of Americana. That one sunk like a lead balloon. Instead, he began experimenting with grouping famous Americans together, for instance Stephen Foster, George Gershwin and Louis Armstrong representing music. One of his pieces struck a nerve, showing Ben Franklin and Mark Twain conversing with Robert Benchley. Marc labeled it "Men of Humor."

After Marc left WED, Randy Bright was given the assignment. Robert Benchley was out, and Will Rogers was in. Bright developed an outline for the show, received approval from Marty Skla and was set to present his idea with script, storyboards and paper dolls to Card Walker.

When the day arrived, Walker arrived at the conference room in terrible back pain and slowly lowered himself onto a stool. As Bright began his pitch, the ordinarily enthusiastic Walker remained cold and silent. Bright thought his presentation was bombing. In a rising panic, Bright began to play out the roles of the show, acting out all of the parts.

When he was finished, Walker said quietly: "It's worth the price of admission to Epcot." Then he stood up and slammed his fist down on the stool: "Goddammit it, it's worth the fucking price of admission to EPCOT!"[146] Bright's *American Adventure* show would go on to be sponsored by American Express and Coca-Cola and is still worth the price of admission.

World Showcase never had the massive corporate benefactors that Future World enjoyed, instead relying on a motley assortment of vendors and alcoholic beverage conglomerates. As it turns out, retailers and beverage

Graffiti on Orange Avenue in Winter Park, circa 1981. *Author's collection.*

distributors tend to want to sponsor shops and restaurants, not attractions, leaving Disney on the hook for almost everything in World Showcase.

The most ambitious World Showcase pavilion was to be Equatorial Africa, with a village, treehouse view of a savanna watering hole at dusk, *Heartbeat of Africa* show and a walk-through "sound safari." A personal favorite of Card Walker, the attraction was cut from the opening day lineup, leaving some African rocks along World Showcase lagoon as the only hint of what could be. A Denmark pavilion was reduced to some Danish-looking bathrooms. The Kingdom of Morocco had failed to produce funds in time for opening day and was similarly represented by some decorated restrooms. A Rhine River Cruise past miniature reproductions of famous German cities was cut from Germany. To this day, the large arches at the rear of the pavilion remain; just past them was intended to be the boarding area for the boat ride.

Tishman Construction newspaper advertisement congratulating Disney on the opening of EPCOT Center, October 1, 1982. *Author's collection.*

The second most elaborate attraction developed for World Showcase was Japan's *Meet the World*, an effort headed up by avowed Nipponophile Claude Coats. Coats's attraction was to be situated inside the massive Japanese castle at the rear of the pavilion. Guests were to enter and climb a staircase to a second level, where the attraction would unfold inside a rotating theater. Audio animatronics interacted with animation produced by a Japanese studio, creating an intriguing intersection between East and West.[147]

At the climax of the show, guests would stand up and exit through a set representing Tokyo's famous Ginza district before winding their way downstairs through exhibits from Japanese companies like Fujifilm and NEC. The 1980s were the height of America's economic panic about Japan's economic power. Despite Japanese products from JVC (VHS), Sony (the Walkman) and Nintendo (the NES, the Game Boy) being zeitgeist-defining bits of tech, Disney upper management worried about their image being tarnished by association.[148] In the end, Disney built *Meet the World* only at Tokyo Disneyland, and the space constructed for the attraction remains empty.

At some point, somebody—probably Dick Nunis—raised the point that there needed to be more to do in World Showcase, and so a cost-reduced version of the Mexico boat ride, called Las Tres Culturas de Mexico, was fast-tracked for opening day. Economically wedged by Claude Coats into existing empty space inside the pavilion,[149] El Rio del Tiempo would be ready for opening day as EPCOT Center's fifth ride-through attraction.

The park opened on time in 1982. National advertisements announced "The 21st Century Begins October 1, 1982." Compared to Magic Kingdom,

EPCOT Center had fewer rides, but what rides! The most impressive Future World pavilions were pretty much entire theme park areas all under one roof. The Universe of Energy was an epic that lasted for three-quarters of an hour, with massive rolling theater cars winding their way across rotating platforms and through a swamp filled with audio-animatronic dinosaurs. The concept was soon copied by touring exhibitions of animated dinosaurs that cropped up in museums and civic centers around the nation.

The World of Motion attraction clocked in at a paltry fifteen minutes— longer than any moving vehicle ride at Magic Kingdom—but those who took the time to take in the exhibition space and two theater shows at the exit could expect to spend a full hour in the clutches of General Motors without having to brave the Floridian humidity.

But the best and most influential had to be Journey Into Imagination, Kodak's attraction. Something like if The Haunted Mansion met It's A Small World, the seventeen-minute tour began with vehicles latching onto a rotating platform and viewing a five-minute stage prologue introducing the

The perfect 1980s family experiences the perfect 1980s fever dream: EPCOT Center. Promotional photo © Disney. *Author's collection.*

characters of the attraction, Dreamfinder and Figment. After exploring Art, Literature, Theater, Science and Motion Pictures, an ancient predecessor of a digital camera took riders' photographs, and they unloaded near the ImageWorks, an exhibition housed upstairs inside the pavilion's glass pyramids. The light, sound and illusion exhibitions found inside were copied at educational and scientific exhibits around the country.

EPCOT's influence was vibrant and short-lived. Popular culture was changing, with teenybopper '80s leading the charge into the youth-oriented 1990s. Technology was changing—a computer that was pretty advanced in 1982 looked hopelessly antiquated by 1988. And Disney was changing.

EPCOT Center grew in the only soil it could have, bloomed briefly and died away. Like the world's fairs it was based on, it was too good to last. But those of us who saw it when it was in its original state will never be able to forget it, and its influence has continued. The twenty-first century really did begin on October 1, 1982.

23

THE HEART OF A CITY

So why did EPCOT die so quickly? There are a few reasons. The 1970s and early '80s were a time when the broader amusement park industry was chasing bigger and flashier thrills. The roller coaster arms race had begun in the 1970s and lasted through the millennium, and every year seemed to bring new boundary-pushing thrills. These market conditions created a new audience, one that had no time for the sedate excitement Disney had offered in the '60s and '70s.

EPCOT, by contrast, was aimed squarely at adults. It had no thrill rides, it served wine and most of the constantly flowing background music sounded like easy listening. Disney zigged while the entire industry zagged, and the immediate payoff was below expectations. When Michael Eisner arrived in the company, he saw Epcot's lack of teenage appeal as something that needed immediate correction.

All of this means that basically nothing of what opened at Epcot in 1982 remains. Unlike almost every other theme park in the country, this park's historical context has been almost wiped clean. This puts a book like this in a difficult position because there is precious little I can direct you to that tells a compelling story. And so, like Disney in the '80s, I'm going to zig while everyone else zags. I'd like to talk about EPCOT's legacy by taking a look at EPCOT's role in the proud American tradition of getting drunk on vacation. You heard me.

Since 1971, Disney had been tasting the money that could be made through the sale of adult beverages at Walt Disney World hotels; in 1975,

Promotional slide © Disney. *Author's collection.*

it expanded the program with the Walt Disney World Village's offerings, which included a deli pouring beers and a seafood bar that served strawberry daiquiris. Tourists were bemused and appreciative, but it was really the Orlando locals who loved the combination of high-class drinking with top-name entertainment.

And so EPCOT Center would be home to fine dining from the very start. I'm not sure but would not be surprised to learn that the entire idea for World Showcase came from a desire to capitalize on this new "wet" revenue stream. Disney found alcohol companies more than willing to partner with a Disney theme park, a realm that had up to now been ruled by the soft drink. Dos Equis signed on for Mexico, Beck's for Germany, Kirin beer for Japan, Bass Ales and Guinness for the United Kingdom and Labatt for Canada. On the wine side, Barton & Guestier represented France, and Schmitt Sohne had a store in Germany. There was a bit of a pattern emerging.

Marking this new era, in January 1982 the Walt Disney World Village hosted its first two-day wine festival. For a fee, 1,500 persons a day could taste California wines from forty-two vintners. Demonstrating that Disney knew its market, discounted overnight packages were available to Florida residents. Within a few years, the event had expanded to one-hundred-plus vintners and was getting significant local press. After eating and drinking

October 1982 Guidebook. *Author's collection.*

their way around the Golden State, attendees walked away with souvenir wine glasses—assuming they could walk at all.

Alongside this brave new world of drinking, EPCOT was developing a bit of a reputation. Thrill-crazed teenagers, of course, continued to stay away, but older folks, single travelers and a certain breed of visitor found the park perfectly suited to their taste. The lack of squalling children and cavorting rodents were significant plusses, not demerits.

Word began to spread that World Showcase presented an opportunity for a truly memorable drinking spree. If I had to guess who invented the practice, I'd point to Disney cast members—they tend to be young, have free access to the park and are legendarily capacious. To drink around the world was still but a whisper, but it was one being heard.

The year 1994 happened to be the final one for Disney's Wine Festival, which by then had expanded to the Beach Club, had a lakeside barbecue, offered seminars all across property and lasted for almost a week. Oenophiles waited out a bitter 1995 with nary a peep of the event, until it returned in 1996 as something called the *Epcot International Food & Wine Festival*. As the name implies, it was now housed at Epcot. And even more importantly, you had to buy your food and wine à la carte while schlepping yourself around a hot theme park.

This fundamentally changed not only the nature of the event but also Epcot itself. At the original wine event, the drinking was hidden out of sight in an inconspicuous conference center, and attendees were exclusively there to sample wines. The drinking was now out in the open, along the main walkway of World Showcase and dispensed like soda pop. And as always, vacations give license to exceptional behavior.

This also corresponded with a broader shift in the role of Epcot at Walt Disney World. Epcot had always been a bit niche, and its role as a foil to Magic Kingdom was muddled by the addition of kid-centric fare to Disney–MGM Studios. Disney closed all of the family-friendly rides at Epcot in the '90s—no more World of Motion, Horizons or Journey Into Imagination—just at the point where they could have begun being recognized as classics. And so the drinking became the most famous thing about Epcot, and people responded by planning their entire day at Epcot around drinking.

But let's take a step back here, because this isn't entirely about the drinking. It's intriguing to consider that Disney theme parks, through the merits of intention or simply selective use, tend to sort themselves into categories based on the order they were built.

Because Disney builds castle parks first, and those tend to be jammed full of high-profile rides, the castle parks tend to be relatively touring-intensive. Epcot was built as counter-programming to that, and despite the fact that Disney has continued to add thrill rides to the park, it is not at all a "ride park."

What matters at Epcot is the quaint pleasure of the boat ride through The Land greenhouses, stopping for a pretzel in Germany and seeing the garden railroad or the Japanese koi pond. It is Disney's first and best hangout park.

And that is exactly how savvy visitors use it. Locals, having long since gotten their fill of Space Mountain, congregate in Epcot to simply relax and enjoy the act of being there. And as architect Charles Moore points out: "What [Disneyland] is all about is inhabitation, the human act of being somewhere where we are protected, even engaged, by a space ennobled by our presence."

This view shows the pleasant "College Campus of the Future" EPCOT originally evoked. *Courtesy of the Lake Buena Vista Historical Society.*

Courtesy of the Lake Buena Vista Historical Society.

So maybe it's time to flip the script on the forty-year-long debate on EPCOT Center, the one where Disney "failed" Walt by building not a city of the future but a theme park. It's certainly just as easy to say that Epcot "fails" to be a theme park… or at least a traditional one.

Most theme parks would close if they lost all their best rides, but this didn't stop Epcot, which has a fanbase that has grown only more devoted with each passing year. So if a theme park is defined as a collection of rides, then maybe Epcot is best defined as *not* a theme park.

So, yes, Disney did not build Epcot as a "city" in Florida, but Epcot nonetheless functions as a civic center. It is a walkable downtown of shops and restaurants filled with Floridians, with a monorail, a lake for boats, constant art festivals and—oh yeah—some rides. It is a jubilant space where people *want* to go, and where they *want* to return to once they've been.

An argument could be made that, just as Angelenos know that Disneyland is Los Angeles's true downtown, then Epcot fulfills the same purpose for Orlando and maybe for all of Florida. It is the center of activity, the best place to see, be seen and celebrate. Isn't that what a city center is supposed to be all about?

Epcot is a city where everyone can be a local. And millions count themselves as citizens.

PART V

THE INCREDIBLE EXPANDING MOUSE

Such a bounty has fallen into my lap.
Every day a new asset falls out of the sky.

–Michael Eisner

24

SUCCESSION

Since December 1971, the Disney company had been run by a coalition of people loosely organized by the board of directors, Donn Tatum, Card Walker and Ron Miller. And these three were driving the company down the road to hell paved with good intentions.

Ironically, the start of the problem goes all the way back to Walt's brother Roy. Roy was determined to open Walt Disney World entirely debt-free. To do this, the Disney Company issued waves of convertible debentures, which is a type of debt that converts to stock after a specified period. This expanded the pool of stockholders so significantly that the percentage of the company owned by the Disney family dwindled from 51 percent to just 7 percent.[150]

Generally speaking, the 1970s were a great time for Disney theme parks and a bad time for Disney movies. This was occurring with the rise of film blockbusters as a backdrop, where Hollywood films like *Jaws*, *Smokey and the Bandit*, *Superman* and *Star Wars* were leapfrogging one another on their way to unprecedented earnings.

The Disney response to these earnings bonanzas were things like *Island at the Top of the World* and *The Black Hole*. Disney's market share of the box office sat at just 4 percent.[151]

The entire company was languishing, paralyzed by Card Walker's inability to spend money on anything not called EPCOT Center. Elliott Gould remembered working with the same mixing and sound equipment purchased four decades ago for *Fantasia*.[152] When the company belatedly

Left to right: Ron Miller, Donn Tatum and Card Walker. *From the 1982 Walt Disney Productions Annual Report*, © *Disney*.

sprang for company cars for the fifty top executives, everybody received the same station wagon. Admission to the theme parks had stayed at pretty much the same price it had been at when Walt Disney died in 1966; you could still ride Pirates of the Caribbean for the same ninety cents. This was occurring at a time in U.S. financial history known as "The Great Inflation."

At the same time, Disney was spending some $1.2 billion on EPCOT Center. The company had taken on massive debt to get the park open, and attendance at EPCOT slipped immediately following its opening.[153] This was at a time when Walt Disney World represented *two-thirds* of the company's revenue.[154] Wall Street was unimpressed. There was blood in the water, and the wolves came out.

At this moment, Roy E. Disney—Roy's son and Walt's nephew—left the board of directors and was exploring a hostile takeover bid of Walt Disney Productions. Roy E. had nearly doubled his wealth through real estate investments with his partner Stanley Gold since leaving Disney in 1977, and his intent was to return that 51 percent share of stock to the Disney family. Just as fundamentally, the nephew (Roy Disney) wanted the son-in-law (Ron Miller) out. Disney and Gold solicited Micheal Milken, a junk bond dealer, who thought he could raise the $2 million required to buy up the stock. But at that cost, huge chunks of the company would have to be sold to recoup the purchase. Roy declined and instead purchased enough stock to give him 5 percent of the company.

To Roy's ire, Milken turned around and made his offer to Saul Steinberg, a corporate raider. Steinberg saw nothing wrong with selling Disney for scraps and launched his own hostile takeover bid in March 1984.

This sent Disney scrambling to find an angel investor to buy up enough stock and keep it out of the hands of Steinberg. It landed on Arvida, a real estate developer owned by billionaire investor Sid Bass. Bass traded Arvida to Disney in exchange for 3.3 million shares, making Bass the largest shareholder in the Walt Disney company at 8.9 percent. The combined shares of Bass and Roy Disney were now enough to prevent Steinberg from taking control. However, this also meant that Roy Disney was no longer the largest shareholder in Disney, and he sued the board of directors. Instead, Roy Disney and his lawyer Stanley Gold were invited to join the board.

With Roy Disney, Stanley Gold and Sid Bass now on the board, all three were aligned against Ron Miller. Miller had delivered *Splash*, the largest hit in the company's history, for Disney. But he had also been behind all of the highest-profile film losses and represented the company's most underperforming division of the last decade—the film division. Another Ron Miller special,[155] *The Black Cauldron*, had been churning through production for years and had cost the company some $44 million. To put this in perspective, this is 400 percent the budget of *Splash* and nearly two-thirds the budget of Epcot Center's most elaborate attraction, Horizons. Miller had also launched The Disney Channel for $82 million, an expected money loser through at least 1986. Somebody had to be the scapegoat, and Ron Miller was definitely somebody.[156]

Roy E. Disney had been positioning Frank Wells to lead the company since his takeover bid began. Wells, in turn, believed the correct leader was Michael Eisner, the flashy Hollywood executive who with Barry Diller had turned around the fortunes of Paramount Pictures. Michael Eisner's claim to fame was approving the deal that Steven Spielberg and George Lucas had sought in making *Raiders of the Lost Ark*. Eisner believed in producing films as cheaply as possible with an emphasis on characters, clear conflicts, tidy resolutions and a "concept" that was easy to market. His roster of hit properties included *Happy Days*, *Grease*, *Flashdance*, *Footloose*, *Beverly Hills Cop* and *48 Hours*. With a shakeup underway at Paramount, Diller and Eisner were parting ways, and the time was right to scoop Eisner up.

Once Sid Bass had been convinced, the board had to vote. The deciding vote in Eisner's favor was placed by Card Walker. By September 1984, the

Courtesy of the Lake Buena Vista Historical Society.

first of many battles of succession to the Kingdom of Disney had been won, and Frank Wells and Michael Eisner were the new Roy and Walt. Eisner and Wells's goals were clear: turn around the movie studio, produce blockbuster hits, make better use of Disney's thirty-seven thousand acres of land in Florida and build more hotels. They got to work.

25

LIGHT SPEED TO ENDOR

I n the summer of 1977, Disney was preparing to release its anticipated summer blockbuster, um, *Herbie Goes to Monte Carlo*. Just ten miles away in a rented warehouse in Van Nuys, a group of inexperienced filmmakers was finishing up the post-production on its very first picture. Members of that group took their name from the warehouse in which they worked and called themselves Industrial Light & Magic. The film, of course, was *Star Wars*. There may be no better example of why Disney needed to clean house at the top than the fact that it put films like *Pete's Dragon* and *Herbie Goes to Monte Carlo* up directly against *Star Wars*.

Yet George Lucas was not entirely foreign to Disney. Lucas had graduated from USC, and like all Angelenos, he was a Disneyland regular. He pitched Disney on an early version of *Star Wars*, and his recommendation of Michael Eisner to the Disney board was instrumental in paving the way for the selection. In a splashy declaration of intent, Eisner immediately approved a platoon of additions to Disneyland: a giant dance club next to It's A Small World and two George Lucas blockbuster attractions called Captain EO and Star Tours.

Star Tours was based on a system by Rediffusion Simulation, a company that produced full-body flight simulators for the defense and aviation industries. Rediffusion called this system the ATLAS, and it was specifically targeted at the amusement park industry. Disney had actually bought the rights years before but, paralyzed by Card Walker's indecisions and budget overruns at EPCOT, had languished. On seeing the concept,

Eisner and George Lucas leapt. With no need to engineer the basic people-carrying mechanism, the ATLAS promised a flashy and relatively fast way to produce a new attraction for Disneyland. After all, motion base aside, the attraction was basically a movie, and Michael Eisner *knew* how to make movies.

The basic concept was nothing new. In the early, experimental days of cinema, George C. Hale invented an attraction known as Hale's Tours.[157] This concept was sold all around the United States on a franchise system. In one of those weird moments of synchronicity, one of the first Hale's Tours locations opened at Walt Disney's childhood amusement park, Electric Park in Kansas City.[158]

Riders at Hale's Tours ascended a staircase to a room decorated like the interior of a train car. The end of the car was open, facing a movie screen. The screen was slightly inclined forward, creating a wrap-around effect. Wheels along the bottom of the room ran across a belt-driven system that simulated the sensation of riding on rails. Films showed points of interest around the world shot from the rear of a train, while an employee dressed as a conductor punched tickets and lectured on the views. In later years, some of these attractions seem to have switched to showing narrative films. One example was *The Hold-Up of the Rocky Mountain Express*, about a train robbery. One wonders if employees dressed as bandidos burst in on patrons during an especially tense moment.

Star Tours was overseen by Tony Baxter and Tom Fitzgerald with George Lucas acting as executive producer. The project came at the right time for Lucas, who had been stepping away from filmmaking since the release of *Return of the Jedi*. Lucas brought fresh eyes to Disney. A trip backstage at Disneyland inspired the attraction's opening thrill, where Captain Rex drives the passenger ship through a maintenance bay. Industrial Light & Magic produced the four-minute film for a cost of $6 million.

Since Eisner had entered Disney, the name of the game at the theme parks had been quick fixes. A national advertising campaign—a concept vehemently opposed by Card Walker—began in 1985, swelling attendance at the parks by 10 percent. Eisner edited the commercials himself.[159] Theme park price increases were ordered immediately, adding some $31 million a year to the company's profits-per-dollar increase.[160] The circus performed at EPCOT, and yearly giveaways of cars at the front gate encouraged multiple trips. The state fair came to Disneyland, with fair food, a Ferris wheel, lumberjack shows and, yes, pig races.[161] Although the promotions would continue, Star Tours marked the end of Eisner's apprentice period

Promotional slide © Disney. *Courtesy of the Lake Buena Vista Historical Society.*

at the parks. A massive, flashy success heralded by a party in which Disneyland stayed open twenty-four hours, Star Tours piloted the course for the future. Disney hadn't been able to generate interest and publicity like this since the opening of Space Mountain in 1975.

Almost instantly, Star Tours became a genre maker. Despite plans to premiere the attraction in Florida at the upcoming Disney-MGM Studios, a variant known as Body Wars was hastily added to the upcoming Wonders of Life pavilion at EPCOT. Leonard Nimoy, who had directed the monster Touchstone hit *Three Men and a Baby*, was tapped as director. This author well remembers waiting in a line that stretched outside the pavilion and almost to the nearby Universe of Energy.

Overnight, every theme park in the country needed an answer to Star Tours. Busch Gardens had Questor, and Sea World debuted Mission: Bermuda Triangle. Movie World Parks in Australia and Germany, backed by Warner Bros., had Batman Adventure: The Ride. Video arcade operators SEGA produced cost-reduced simulators appropriate for malls. A few McDonald's locations bought ATLAS systems and marketed the attraction as the "McThriller." Universal Studios, which likes to be different, developed its own motion platform systems and debuted The Funtastic World of Hanna-Barbera and Back to the Future: The Ride.

Star Tours under construction at the Disney-MGM Studios in 1989. *Courtesy of the Lake Buena Vista Historical Society.*

And Star Tours initiated another important development, which was the gradual drawing together of Disney and Lucasfilm. In the late '90s, Disney bid on the release rights for Lucas's prequel trilogy, but it was widely known that 20th Century Fox under no circumstances would let those movies go.[162] But following the end of that series, *Star Wars* and Disney increasingly blurred.

Star Wars Weekend, which began in 1997, expanded until it was more like "Star Wars Month." Disney characters dressed as *Star Wars* characters increasingly flooded merchandise shops; Darth Goofy and Minnie Leia became surreal companions to Snow White and Perry the Platypus all through the late 2000s. All of this culminated in the outright purchase of Lucasfilm in 2012, a $4 billion expenditure that was recouped after just two movies.

Today, Disneyland and Hollywood Studios are home to lavish, cutting-edge *Star Wars* areas that share park space with Star Tours, the original beachhead that gradually drew these two entertainment juggernauts together. Michael Eisner's big declaration of intent changed the industry forever.

26

HOLLYWOOD EAST!

Florida's mogul recruiters like to boast that the state can provide everything but mountains, which sounds great—most filmmakers don't need mountains. But no filmmaker needs two weeks of rain, and Florida couldn't do much for the Porky's II *people when the state delivered just that.*
—*Bill Cosford,* Miami Herald, *July 4, 1982*[163]

Hollywood has a tradition called the "thirty-mile zone." This is an area extending out from the center of the film production capital roughly thirty miles in each direction that is, for the purposes of budgeting and union rates, considered to be "within driving distance." The zone stretches from Santa Clarita through the Santa Monica Mountains and includes Long Beach, Disneyland (which was originally intended to double as a backlot) and a good chunk of Los Angeles National Forest. If you've ever been to Los Angeles, you know that this represents an amazingly diverse array of locations, from beachside Santa Monica to rural Topanga Canyon and urban downtown. With set dressing and camera angles, you can create the effect of films set almost anywhere within the reasonable limits of this zone.

And that is the easiest way to explain why film production in Florida has simply never taken off. A Florida beach doesn't look too different than the ones at Long Beach or outside San Diego, and the inland part of Florida speaks more to old South than anything else.

And yet to this day, a significant number of Floridians still believe that there is a chance that one day Florida would be "Hollywood East." For that we can thank Florida governor Bob Graham, who served the state from 1979 until 1987. Graham made a point and more than a bit of a political show of his vision, and by the early '80s, there was a small rash of film production occurring in the Sunshine State. The ones you may remember are *Body Heat* and *Porky's*; the ones nobody remembers are *Honky Tonk Freeway*, *Hardly Working*, *Porky's II* and *Nobody's Perfect*. Alas.

Yet all of this was perfectly timed for Eisner and his studio head Jeffrey Katzenberg, who had been steadily working to undo a decade of financial lethargy by producing low-budget, high-concept comedies. Eisner called this strategy "singles and doubles" (as opposed to "home runs"). Fare like *Down and Out in Beverly Hills*, *Stakeout*, *Ernest Goes to Camp*, *Ruthless People* and *Cocktail* may not be well remembered today, but these were successful money spinners that began to build Disney back up to be able to tackle more ambitious fare.

And then of course there was The Disney Channel, which was losing subscribers almost as quickly as it got them and needed more new programming, fast. Disney's Florida property promised low cost and existing infrastructure and suddenly began to make sense as a venue to expand production capacity.

And so Disney announced that it intended to build a movie studio in Orlando in 1985. The Disney-MGM Studio, set to open in 1988, seemed to make good on Bob Graham's promise to turn Florida into a production mecca; on the strength of this political windfall, Graham would shortly launch a bid for the U.S. Senate.[164] Eisner predicted at the announcement: "Both the lion and the mouse will roar."[165] Central Floridians were bristling with excitement. And then, almost nothing happened.

I have in my collection a remarkable booklet published to sell moviemakers on the Disney-MGM Studios as a viable location. The booklet breaks down Florida weather, local population demographics, scenery around town and the benefits of Walt Disney World itself—scenic and machine shops, restaurants, catering, luxury hotels. It points out that shooting inside Walt Disney World requires no fees or permits; the entire resort is a huge backlot. The book ends with a tour of Disney's seven-building production hub with its three soundstages, editing suites, screening rooms, ADR and Foley booths and even a satellite uplink for sending dailies off to Los Angeles. Eisner comments in a written foreword: "We knew a total commitment would have to be made in order to provide you with the finest production facilities ever built anywhere. We hope you'll bring some of your productions here in the

© Disney. *Author's Collection.*

future, and discover why the Disney-MGM Studios are the best place to produce in the world."

And at first, the new movie studio was a success at drawing productions. *Superboy*, a low-budget television spinoff of the successful film franchise, used Walt Disney World and the University of Central Florida as its backlot. The immortal *Ernest Saves Christmas* was completed, as was *Splash Too*[166] and a revival of the *Mickey Mouse Club*. The studio backlot consisted of a suburban street with houses in a variety of styles and a "city street" that never quite became anything other than New York. The city street set was put up to film *The Lottery*, a two-minute film starring Bette Midler.[167]

But competition was brewing. Universal Orlando opened its studio facilities in 1990, with four full-sized soundstages to Disney's one and a half. Almost instantly, *Superboy* moved up the interstate to larger facilities. It was an ominous portent.[168] As it turned out, *Ernest Saves Christmas* was the sole theatrical feature filmed at Disney's Florida studio. Part of the trouble was the theme park part of the facility once it opened in May 1989; just to the south of the backlot area was Catastrophe Canyon, a special effects show that regularly detonated explosions. Immediately to the north was the *Indiana Jones Epic Stunt Spectacular*, which also had multiple explosions. With both shows running simultaneously—and they were among the most popular in the park—any outdoor shooting quickly became impossible.

Disney created plastic replicas of motion picture film cameras and left them around the backlot set to give the illusion that filming was occurring. Universal Studios' Terry Winnick visited the Disney park during a cast member preview day and observed the sets for *Superboy* standing but not operating.[169] Disney shot a few scenes from *Honey, I Blew Up the Kid* at the studio, but the big draw in that case was Disney's Merchandise Distribution Center, large enough for the scene where the shrink ray is recovered from a warehouse.

The only other example I can find of a theatrical feature even attempting to use the Disney Backlot after May 1989 is the mob comedy *Oscar*. Apparently, on arriving at the location, director John Landis declared the New York Street set entirely unusable, and the production moved up the street to Universal Studios Florida. Alas.[170]

It's not fair to say that the studio facility was a total failure. Disney, at least, continued to use the Florida facilities for television production until the late '90s. But attracting other production companies turned out to be a pipe dream. With a shift in content strategy at the top of the company, the extra

Tourists look down into the set for the *MMC* television program, 1989. Promotional photo © Disney. *Courtesy of the Lake Buena Vista Historical Society.*

space was not needed. As it turned out, it was hard to get enough people to move out to Florida to make the cost savings effective.

Honey, I Blew Up the Kid producer Edward Feldman told the *Orlando Sentinel*: "If it weren't for the trams going, I think you would get a lot of big pictures here. The big-time directors have a difficult time turning around and seeing trams behind them and glass walls."[171] The soundstages built for production now house Toy Story Mania, with the surrounding facilities and backlot having been leveled in 2016 to make way for Stars Wars: Galaxy's Edge.

In the end, Universal got the job done that Disney failed to. Home to a constant stream of production since opening in 1990, Universal now has seven soundstages on-site, with the park area built to proper backlot standards plus a small area for outdoor filming. The facilities are kept busy with small productions, television shows and wrestling matches. It may not be, well, "Hollywood" East, but it's a real movie studio. No plastic cameras needed.

27

HURRY UP AND BUILD—AGAIN

So that's the story of the back half of the Florida Studio; what about the front half?

Disney-MGM—now called Hollywood Studios—is a strange, confusing park. In other Disney parks, like Magic Kingdom or Epcot, pathways wind inevitably toward the next destination. You rarely have to make a choice or backtrack. The Studios Park, in contrast, is filled with baffling cul-de-sacs and dead ends. Almost as if it wasn't meant to be a theme park…

The story actually begins with Universal Studios out in Hollywood. Since 1964, Universal had been running trams through its legendary backlot, the last one still standing since the days of silent film. Trams would bring riders past costume and scenic shops, sets of movie houses (including the Munster house) and celebrity bungalows.

The tour stopped halfway through to allow visitors to get out, stretch their legs and wander around a "prop plaza" before heading on to such attractions as *Jaws* and a flash flood. As the tour grew in popularity, Universal began adding facilities around its entrance like cafeterias, a western stunt show and a demonstration of special effects.

By the late '70s, Universal was looking to expand into Florida. It ended up buying most of the Florida Center land, finally bringing the circle to a close as what was once touted as the site of a city of the future became yet another theme park.[172] However, Universal head Lew Wasserman was shy of the financial risk and went shopping for a partner. Universal and

Paramount had launched the USA Television Network together in 1980, so their first stop was Paramount, run by Barry Diller,[173] Michael Eisner and Jeffrey Katzenberg.

The meeting of the minds occurred on July 29, 1981, at Universal. Diller, Eisner and others were shown plans for a park that included a Hollywood-style street of shops, a water ride, a "Screen Tester Theater" and sound effects show and a transplanted version of the California studio tour.[174] Paramount demurred. Universal brought the show to multiple other companies, including RCA and, tellingly, Sid Bass. Bass, never one to sit on a lead, got into bed with Disney six months later. Of course, Disney contested these charges loudly. Perhaps a bit too loudly.[175]

Frustrated, Universal's Jay Stein went on an anti-publicity tour about the theft. Speaking to the *Los Angeles Times*, he asserted that "65% to 70% of the elements on Disney's tour are 'borrowed' from Universal's 1981 plans." Stein went on:

> *I just think that when you work as hard as we did in trying to get this program and studio tour off the ground—and this is a project I have worked on for 20 years—you see someone come along and take your ideas and incorporate them in their project and say that this was their idea.... That just makes me angry.*[176]

Draw your own conclusions, but the fact remains that Disney's announcement of its own Studio Tour attraction in Florida represented a gauntlet thrown. Having thus put its competitor on notice, Disney had to move fast. If Universal projected it would take four to five years to put up its planned attraction, Eisner wanted it ready in three. The intent was to dissuade Universal from entering the Orlando market at all.

The size of the park was intentionally constricted to avoid the cost overruns of EPCOT Center. The Studio park would be situated at the intersection of two existing roads, requiring minimal infrastructure to get it open. The park is literally wedged between three roads and its own parking lot. Disney wanted it *yesterday*.

So what awaited visitors inside the newest Disney theme park in 1989? Not much, is the answer. Upon arrival, guests would walk down Hollywood Boulevard just as they do now, arriving at the familiar hub-like area in front of the Chinese Theater. There were now two options: left or right. If you headed right, you would be leaving the "theme park" area and passing into the "working studio" portion of the park. This is why there is inexplicably a second entrance arch to the right of the Chinese Theater with the park's name on it.

Behind the arch was the park's killer attraction: the two-hour studio tour. Trams would bring riders past costume and scenic shops, past sets of movie houses (including the *Golden Girls* house) and into Catastrophe Canyon. The trams would then head down the New York street set from *The Lottery* and deposit guests at a "production plaza" where they could wander around shops. If all of this sounds familiar, you're on the right track.

The second half of the tour included a water tank, demonstration of miniatures, blue screen effects, soundstages, editing and finally a theater where previews of upcoming films could be seen.

If you headed left instead of right at the Chinese Theater, you could take a walk around Echo Lake, designed to resemble Los Angeles in the 1950s befitting its television-focused offerings. The key attraction here was *Superstar Television* and *Monster Sound Show*, two audience participation shows. Opening later was the Indiana Jones stunt show and, in its own little side area called the "Backlot Annex," Star Tours.

Almost instantly, the park was a success, but its tiny size meant it was hardly capable of dealing with the demand it had created. Everybody wanted to see Catastrophe Canyon, but almost nobody understood it was just one part of a massive two-hour attraction. More of everything was needed, fast.

Hollywood Boulevard in 1990. *Courtesy of the Lake Buena Vista Historical Society.*

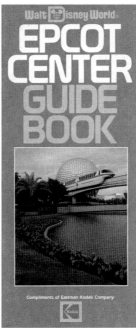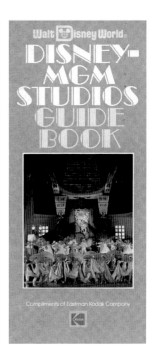

Souvenir guide maps for all three parks, circa May 1989. *Author's collection.*

A Muppets area was hastily added to the back of the "Backlot Annex," crammed up against the side of the New York street set. This created a bottleneck with only one point of entry, forcing Disney to open the New York set to pedestrian traffic. An area formerly used as a tram turnaround became a small pathway back to the Chinese Theater. The trams now proceeded halfway down the New York set, then looped down the side "San Francisco" street and back to the "production plaza." This didn't help the people desperately wandering around trying to find Catastrophe Canyon; now they could see the trams but couldn't get onto them!

So Disney accepted the inevitable and split the Studio Tour into two attractions: the tram tour and the walking "Effects Tour." The trams now merely glimpsed the New York set because guests could walk all the way down it to the production plaza and see the coveted *Splash Too* fountain. This inevitably resulted in the Effects Tour being cut and cut until it was merely a series of disconnected walkthrough diversions.

Amazingly, Disney kept this arrangement for almost twenty-five years. The Studios consisted of four areas that were basically a theme park and a confusing warren of cul-de-sacs and dead ends at the rear of the place. Finally, tired of forcing guests to circumnavigate a giant outdoor set constructed for a two-minute Bette Midler movie in the Reagan administration, Disney leveled the entire rear of the park in 2016.

Universal came to town anyway. Disney's industrial larceny had inspired Universal to hit back by enlarging and improving its park to be a serious rival to Disney. Universal Studios Florida almost instantly began to siphon guests from EPCOT, forcing Disney to spend money it wasn't prepared to spend to keep EPCOT competitive. Universal disrupted the industry just as Disneyland did in 1955.

28

THE FATAL PERRIER BOTTLE

In March 1985, Michael Eisner held a "futurist conference" at the Contemporary Resort. This was really a fancy way of saying "planning committee for how to spend our money." Over the course of two days, a plan emerged. The future of Walt Disney World was hotels.

Eisner and Katzenberg had each taken vacations to Orlando—Eisner actually had to be dissuaded from driving a Winnebago, Griswold-like, from Los Angeles in order to "get into the head of the average tourist." Both found that the nearly twenty thousand hotel rooms that had sprouted up on the front doorstep were charging more for less. Sid Bass was right. They needed more hotels.

The solution seemed clear. Disney needed to build an average of one thousand hotel rooms a year for the next five years.[177] It began with the Caribbean Beach, a sprawling fifty-acre complex. The screams of protest of area hoteliers were drowned out by the humming of busy construction. And the construction shovels did not stop turning for the next *eighteen years*.

Faced with being thrown into a realm he had no experience in—real estate development—Eisner did what he always did in those days: he got smart, and then he got ambitious. Disney entered negotiations with Marriott to build a dozen hotels through the '90s; after drawing out the negotiations for seven months, Eisner withdrew. He had seen enough of Marriott's operation to know that Disney and Arvida had more than enough experience to do it themselves.[178]

Michael Eisner at the construction of the Walt Disney World Swan. *Courtesy of the Lake Buena Vista Historical Society.*

Tishman, still rattling around the Disney ecosystem after building EPCOT Center, rode herd on the Grand Floridian—an impressive hotel complex planned for the Seven Seas Lagoon. But Tishman's attention to detail was not Disney's attention to detail. The Grand Floridian's execution was below standard.[179] What was worse, Tishman was expecting to build a massive hotel and convention center in Lake Buena Vista; its uninspired design kept Eisner awake for a week.[180] Michael Eisner didn't want just any hotels. He wanted Disney's hotels to look like nothing else in the world, and boy, was he going to get it.

While Eisner pulled strings to terminate Tishman's contract, he began to reach out to his well-heeled circle of influence to find a suitably outré architect. Around this time, Eisner reportedly told an executive at Tishman, "I'm 45 years old. I've made more money than I ever dreamed of. Now I want to be on the cover of *Time* magazine. By using the most controversial architects in the country, I will establish Disney as a serious patron of the arts."[181]

Determined to find something surprising and even provocative, Eisner met architects Philip Jonson and Robert Graves during intermission at the New York City Ballet. Jonson excused himself to get a Perrier, leaving the field open to Graves.[182] Prompted by Eisner to create something outrageous, Graves designed an enormous mountain, nearly three hundred feet tall, rising from the Florida scrub.

Informed he needed to "lighten it up," Graves added bowl fountains, Italianate fish and graceful swans. The twin hotels became the Walt Disney World Swan and Dolphin, as bold an architectural statement as can be imagined. The imposing tropical pink edifices would be painted with teal rocks and crashing waves. Dan Marino, "Florida's premiere dolphin," was on hand for the ceremonial hoisting of the fish onto their perches atop the roof.[183]

Hotel interiors combined bizarre, puffy circus tent motifs with cavorting animals and rockwork. It was either daring and whimsical or distractingly stupid depending on your perspective. The *Orange County Register* hit the nail on the head when Kitty Morgan wrote, "It's as if they took an architect, gave him a hallucinogen, and asked him to design the kind of hotel he would have liked to stay in when he was 12 years old." I'm pretty sure that was meant as a compliment.

In maybe the most Michael Eisner moment in a life full of them, in January 1990, Eisner entered the Walt Disney World Dolphin and announced, with great ceremony, the next ten years of expansions for Disney: The Disney Decade. He announced new theme parks for Florida and California, unspecified swaths of hotels and almost thirty new attractions. Few of these would come to fruition and almost none in the form announced in 1990. Still, the pace of hotel construction did not decline. Robert Stein's colossal Yacht and Beach Club complexes complemented the ostentatious Graves hotels to form a small resort complex of cartoonish exaggeration just outside Epcot. The remote Port Orleans and Dixie Landings were built at the same time as a new timeshare, swelling the available rooms near the Walt Disney World Village by almost two thousand. The All-Star Resorts came online in 1994, directly competing with motels along 192 at Disney's front doorstep. And that's just the ones that opened in the first four years of the 1990s!

Growing up going to Disney World in the '90s, it was easy to take this pace of construction for granted. Every other year, my family would return to find another massive hostelry, and more often than not, they would be inspired. Occasionally, they were more than inspired, such as the case of Wilderness Lodge, which must be one of the most remarkable public spaces in the United States. Had Wilderness Lodge been built anyplace else at any other time it would have been an instant classic; in 1994 at Disney World, it became merely a cult favorite. It's telling that Disney built so much room inventory under Michael Eisner that only recently has it had to finally start looking at developing entirely new properties.

Not all of Michael's ideas were winners. In 1985, the *New York Times* observed: "Among Eisner's far-out ideas is that of a new Chautauqua to make Disney World a cultural center. 'Remember what Plato said some time ago,' he says. [???] 'Let early education be a sort of amusement; you will then be better able to find out the natural bent.'"[184]

In its early days, Disney-MGM placed a priority on making good on being a "Hollywood experience" by strongly emphasizing the entertainment of the day. There was a visiting celebrity program, and shows and entertainment cycled through much more regularly than they have since the turn of the millennium. This resulted in some obvious tie-ins like a parade that changed yearly to reflect Disney Animation's new release as well as some truly bizarre offerings.

For instance, the park hosted a Teenage Mutant Ninja Turtles stage show, a food court themed to the Bette Midler film *Big Business* and even a short-lived stunt show starring Ace Ventura. Dick Tracy apprehended gangsters on the Streets of America. Hulk Hogan starred in WCW wrestling bouts shot in front of the theme park gates. Ellen DeGeneres opened a bookshop. But the height of incongruous has to have been Goosebumps Horrorland, a short "freak show" on stage followed by a brief walk-through experience ending at a gift shop. This overlay unfortunately resulted in the dismantling of the *Who Framed Roger Rabbit* gag factory shop, one of the coolest things in old-school Disney-MGM.

This "New Chautauqua" manifested in the form of the Disney Institute. The press and public at large were plenty confused by this whole "Institute" thing. In 1993, the *Orlando Sentinel* reported that planned activities include an animation class, film production, touring a nature preserve and going to a spa. Those of you taking notes at home will see that all of these activities were things already built at Walt Disney World by Michael Eisner, and despite the talk of "enrichment vacations," it was

Sophisticated adults learning to cook at the Disney Institute. *Courtesy of the Lake Buena Vista Historical Society.*

becoming more than a little easy to guess that that whole "Chautauqua" thing was less than meets the eye.

The cloud of confusion that settled over the Disney Institute never entirely abated. What was finally unveiled in 1996 was basically a rebranded version of the Lake Buena Vista Villas. A new "campus" area included a theater, classrooms, outdoor concert venue and a spa. Disney went all-in on the promotion, producing infotainment planning videos, broadcasting multiple episodes of the Disney Channel program *Inside/Out* from the hotel and even subjecting viewers of the 1995 Walt Disney World Christmas Day Parade to the sight of Joan Lunden rock climbing.[185]

The public stayed away in droves. Confusion persisted on whether families could stay at the Disney Institute without taking place in the programs. The whole thing was too weird and required too much explaining. The hotel closed in 2003 and was mostly demolished to make way for the Saratoga Springs Resort.

But that was a rare misstep for Eisner. I don't think it's unfair to say that Eisner was far better at building hotels than he was at building theme parks. Hotels made money from day one, and unlike in other areas at Disney, Eisner was willing to pay for the best money could buy.

Disney Institute "Visitor Program." *Author's collection.*

Between 1985 and 2001, Disney built an astonishing twenty-five hotels in Orlando, Paris and California. Under Eisner, Walt Disney World transformed from a theme park complex with some hotel rooms supporting it to a hotel complex with some theme parks supporting it. The business of making pleasure was fundamentally transformed.

29

TENNIS BALLS AND CHOCOLATE BARS

A s you may have noticed by now, Michael Eisner was kind of a big weirdo. A Manhattan blueblood who grew up on Park Avenue— his film ethos at Paramount was "no rural and no snow"—Eisner seemed to hold deep inside him a fascination with the "just folks" he addressed from the other side of the movie screen.

You can say a lot about Eisner—believe me, I do—but it's impossible to deny that the man was driven to use the resources of Disney to do something more than simply entertain. Michael Eisner perceived the Disney theme parks not simply as revenue generators but as locations central to the American identity. No creative idea could be too good for them. And of Eisner's pet obsessions, few were as baffling as his obsession with factories. In a profile by the *New York Times Magazine* in 1985, we learn:

> *Eisner* [is] *contemplating the revenues Disney might take in by adding a new, more serious attraction to Disney World—the Industrial Kingdom, where people would ride through working factories and watch park employees making chocolate bars, golf clubs, stuffed animals or breakfast cereals.*
>
> *"This would be the '60 Minutes' of our network schedule," he said. "I think people feel after a week of frivolousness they will come to '60 Minutes' and be cleansed. Before you leave Walt Disney World, you can show your American family how the workplace works."* [186]

Eisner wrote of his lifelong passion for assembly lines in his autobiography *Work in Progress*: "Watching as razor blades were being manufactured in my grandfather's factory during my youth mesmerized me. For some reason, I've always found drama in assembly lines—the excitement of watching products take shape."[187]

"The Workplace" could be seen as pure folly, but the idea kept cropping up in interviews. Bit by bit, the idea was making headway. In the early days of the Eisner administration, where Disney seemed to be finding pots of gold below every bush, nothing seemed to be impossible. But good times would not last.

The Workplace was announced as part of Disney's planned community Celebration in April 1991, grouped together with the Disney Institute. The Workplace was described as a display of "the creative ingenuity of industrial wizards worldwide...making everything from tennis balls to compact discs."[188]

This version of the idea was the nearest Eisner's dreams of factory tours ever got to feasibility. The factories of The Workplace, and the vacation-oriented activities at the Institute, would have meant that Celebration would have opened with an in-built economic revenue stream, something it still doesn't really have today. All of these bold ideas inevitably remind one of Walt Disney's original plans for the property, which pointedly included both a living city and an industrial park.[189]

However, by 1992 the Disney Institute had been decoupled from Celebration. No more was ever heard of The Workplace, with its breakfast cereals, tennis and/or golf balls and compact discs.

Still, dreams of Industrial Kingdoms lingered. Proposed for the controversial Disney's America project was a steel coaster "themed to the Industrial Revolution." The theming consisted of a standard looping steel coaster darting in and out of a factory. The example of The Workplace had been instructive, and Imagineering figured out how to catch Eisner's attention. Instead of fantastical kingdoms or impossible realities, throughout the 1990s, Disney attractions would be set in such locations as The Dino Institute or the Tomorrowland Convention Center—places corporate executives could imagine escaping to unwind.

At long last, Michael Eisner got his dream at Disney's California Adventure, which opened with two factory tours: The Boudin Sourdough Bakery and the Mission Tortilla Factory. California Adventure was generally disliked—it was a common crack in Disney fan circles that Florida got Mission: Space while California got Mission Tortilla. Despite this, the tortilla factory and bakery were among the best-reviewed attractions in the park.

Downtown Celebration in 1996. *Courtesy of the Lake Buena Vista Historical Society.*

Indeed, most of the early version of California Adventure has been removed, but the Boudin Bakery tour remains a stalwart of the park. Turns out people are very interested in "the excitement of watching products take shape." Maybe Eisner's dreams of vacationing families staring longingly at industrial assembly lines of tennis balls or stuffed animals isn't as outrageous as it seems.

30

THE MCMERGER

You may have driven past it and never noticed, but there is a McDonald's on Disney property. It sits all alone out by Blizzard Beach and Animal Kingdom. We drive past McDonald's locations so often in the real world that the incongruity may not have been immediately obvious. But it's not like McDonald's can just buy out the land—Disney had to put it there. So what is exactly one lone McDonald's doing way out in such an odd spot?

The story goes back, as so many of them in this section do, to the early days of the Eisner regime. Sent on a mission to find undercapitalized resources inside the company, Team Disney was delighted to find millions and millions in intellectual property that the Walker and Miller regimes had barely touched. "Everywhere we look we find another couple of hundred million dollars," Eisner enthused to Michael Ovitz while skiing in Colorado.[190]

Disney had been cautious in licensing out its characters for merchandise— just about the only Disney clothes available were a line of Winnie-the-Pooh children's apparel sold at Sears. Eisner's team opened the spigot to the torrent of Disney bric-a-brac that we all float in today, and fast-food promotions were absolutely not off the table.

McDonald's debuted the Happy Meal back in 1979. The very first movie to leverage the kids' meal to promote itself was *Star Trek: The Motion Picture* in 1979 (kids love V'ger!). *Star Trek* was a Paramount film headed up by, guess who, Michael Eisner and Jeffrey Katzenberg.

Interior of a typical McDonald's in 1979, the year the Happy Meal was unleashed. *Library of Congress.*

If it worked for Dr. Spock, it would definitely work for Mickey Mouse. Disney and McDonald's cranked up the promotional machine in 1987 and never looked back. The Golden Arches promoted such touchstones of the era as *DuckTales*, *Who Framed Roger Rabbit* and *The Little Mermaid*. These promotions made it rain money.

But at some point in 1990, the relationship between Disney and McDonald's got a little rocky. Newspapers made much of an apparent split between the companies, fueled by the disappointing reception of *Dick Tracy*. Often overlooked is the fact that Disney-McDonald's Happy Meals continued apace all through this, simply with slightly more niche subjects such as EPCOT or Disneyland's 45th Anniversary.

It's true that Disney ended up partnering with Burger King for the extremely lucrative releases of *Aladdin*, *Lion King* and *Toy Story*.[191] Burger King's acquisition of the tie-in rights to *Lion King* was an absolute bonanza for the restaurant, with the toys selling out so quickly that Burger King had to rush a line of finger puppets into production. Sales of the Burger King kids' meals doubled during the craze.[192] The Golden Arches must have been red with envy.

But the 1990s were an uncertain time for McDonald's. The restaurant had gone in big on marketing to children all through the '70s and '80s, which led to a perception of the restaurant as being "for children." This was not surprising when almost every McDonald's had an enormous playground on its front lawn and interiors featuring kid-size stools with googly-eyed hamburger seats.

This single-minded focus had left the door open for competitors like Burger King and Wendy's to swoop in and compete on quality. McDonald's had painted itself into a corner. The kiddie demographic wanted burgers and shakes. All efforts to expand the menu—McSpaghetti, the McRib, the McDLT, even the McPizza—fell flat.

McDonald's attempted a hail Mary play in 1996 with the launch of the "Arch Deluxe." Launched with a singing and dancing Ronald McDonald at the Radio City Music Hall, McDonald's took a cue from the Sega Genesis marketing playbook and tried to woo adults with marketing insisting that "kids hate the Arch Deluxe!" When children responded to these advertisements by deciding to stop requesting trips to McDonald's, the chain went into panic mode.

Things weren't going much better over at Disney. Frank Wells had died in a tragic accident on Easter 1994. Michael Eisner had a heart attack in July. Jeffrey Katzenberg had very publicly left the company in August 1994, drawing the studio into an ugly swirl of controversy. There were very real discussions about shutting Disneyland Paris, and the residents of Prince William County, Virginia, were up in arms about Disney's proposed historical theme park outside of Williamsburg.

All of the sudden, Disney had lost its most important asset: its public image. Eisner brought in his best friend Michael Ovitz to replace Katzenberg, itself a venture doomed to failure. But Ovitz did manage to engineer an exclusivity agreement between McDonald's and Disney. Perhaps the two ailing family brands could help each other. The partnership was announced in 1996 by Michael Eisner as "a true McDisney production."

McDonald's signed with Disney to sponsor not a restaurant, not an attraction but an *entire area* of Disney World's fourth theme park. This would become Dinoland USA, home to Countdown to Extinction, Animal Kingdom's biggest thrill ride upon opening. Most of Animal Kingdom was less than meets the eye upon opening, but Dinoland was one of the few fully realized areas, and one wonders how much the golden pocketbooks built on french fries assured that.

Placed in the center of Dinoland was not the entrance to an attraction but Restaurantosaurus, a sprawling complex "featuring McDonald's Selections." Yes, for the very first time you could buy a Big Mac inside a Disney theme park. The price of these familiar treats being significantly higher than they were in "real life" did not seem to deter diners.

And that was just the start. Since the '80s, the Walt Disney World Village had been through a number of expansions and identity crises and by the late '90s was known as Downtown Disney. Downtown Disney received its own standalone McDonald's, known as "Ronald McDonald's Playhouse."

EPCOT Center McDonald's toys from 1994. *Author's collection.*

Inside, an aerial conveyance shuffled Happy Meal boxes around above the service counter. A side dining room featured a loft with a french fry organ. The restaurant's opening featured Mary-Kate and Ashley Olsen, for those of you filling out your 1990s bingo cards at home.

And then there was the massive standalone restaurant out by the All-Stars Resorts. Rather than being any sort of comment on the dining habits of those staying at the value resorts—no judgment here, I promise—Disney simply situated the restaurant at the largest freeway interchange that existed at the time on its property.

Nobody who saw this McDonald's in its original incarnation has ever forgotten it. The exterior was hung with titanic versions of the Happy Meal characters that seemed to burst forth from a three-story-tall Happy Meal box. Even for the 1990s—the era that tolerated the Rainforest Cafe—this was extreme. Two years later, McDonald's french fries began being sold at locations around Walt Disney World and Disneyland. Theme park purists cried foul, but because these fries were significantly better than the ones Disney was selling, lines remained long.

But the downfall of McDonald's public image that began in the early '90s could not be avoided, as a variety of events in the early 2000s came together to give the restaurant a reputation only slightly better than that of plutonium smugglers. Despite the supersized controversy, Disney stuck with McDonald's for the duration of their contract. This meant that McDonald's was stuck promoting such expensive Disney flops as *Atlantis* and *Treasure*

The legendary All-Star McDonald's in its original state. *Photo by Stephen Johnson, BuildABetterMouseTrip.com.*

Mid-'90s souvenir maps. *Author's collection.*

Island. This author remembers the heady days of the early 2000s and Disney fan petitions to drop McDonald's as a corporate partner.

By 2007, times were obviously different, and the two brands separated. McDonald's went through a decade of decline as the children's audience it had so actively cultivated in the '80s and '90s grew up into adults who would not be caught dead eating a Quarter Pounder. The french fry kiosks vanished from the theme parks, as did the location at Downtown Disney. Today, only the location out by the All-Star Resorts remains.

Well, almost. Take a ride on Countdown to Extinction / Dinosaur, the thrill ride that Ronald built. In the attraction's boarding area, there are pipes running along the ceiling. One is painted red, one is painted white and the other is painted yellow. These are not only the colors of Ronald McDonald, but each pipe also has a chemical formulation written on it that corresponds to ketchup, mayonnaise and mustard.

31

THE MOUSE THAT ROARED

W alt Disney World's big marketing push for 1996 and 1997 was "Remember the Magic," a highly effective event commemorating the property's twenty-fifth anniversary. It was the definitive Eisner marketing blowout: a television special, catchy pop tune, raft of celebrity guests and headline-catching overlay of Cinderella Castle. But the twenty-fifth anniversary also closed the book on a certain era at Walt Disney World, meaning this book must wrap up its story.

Already under construction was Disney's Animal Kingdom, a massive zoological park. People noticed that this was cutting awfully close to what Busch Gardens in Tampa was already offering. Like the man says, once could be happenstance, twice could be coincidence but three times is a trend. After building its own competitors to Universal Studios (Disney-MGM), Wet 'n Wild (Typhoon Lagoon) and Church Street Station (Pleasure Island), Disney's intent here was unmissable.

What was more, Disney had announced yet another bold new venture: its own cruise line. Dick Nunis had noticed that some families chose to vacation in South Florida due to Miami's cruise terminal; it was one more market to bring home to Orlando.[193] Successfully combining family fun with heady luxury, Disney Cruise Line would come to dominate its corner of the cruise ecosystem.

And thus Walt Disney World stood poised to enter the new millennium in a state hardly recognizable from just fifteen years before. Since Eisner had entered the company, Disney had built two theme parks, two water parks, a

The equally legendary "Castle Cake." *Author's collection.*

sports complex, a nightclub district, four miniature golf courses, two regular golf courses, an entire town in Osceola County, three shopping complexes, a few office buildings and a staggering fifteen hotel complexes just on its property in Florida.

This created more problems than expected. As it turns out, Animal Kingdom did *not* inspire tourists to either forego Universal Studios or add a fifth day to their Disney vacations; they simply split a vacation day between two parks. This fact has held true for a quarter century now. As it turns out, American vacation time and money is relatively inelastic. This is the same folly that threw off Disney's numbers when building a theme park in Europe: it expected Disneyland Paris to make money the way Walt Disney World did (as it turns out, Europeans take longer vacations but spend less money to make up the difference). Animal Kingdom permanently stretched Walt Disney World's resources too thin.

Which pretty much brings us to today. There truly is more at Walt Disney World than anyone can possibly see in one trip. Whether that's the root cause of the resort's vaunted 35 percent return rate is up for debate. Very, very few vacation destinations have more than two theme parks, and Walt Disney World is an example of why. It's hard to add to one of those parks without pulling visitors from the other three.

As the parks have gotten busier in the past quarter century, this has become a frenzied game of whack-a-mole, except with billions of dollars of capital expenditure. It's become a numbers game, not at all about building entertainment or even optimizing spending but simply trying to keep ahead of the curve. Disney has only in the past decade truly begun to push out beyond the boundaries of the box Michael Eisner built for it. The "Disney Decade" turned out to be a quarter-century plan.

But Disney had done it. It had swallowed the American vacation whole.

BACK TO THE PAST

It was a hot July morning when I drove my rental car down Hotel Plaza Boulevard, past the massive mall that once upon a time was called the Walt Disney World Village, past the tiny spit of land where Phil Smith lived alone with his family in the damp Florida wilderness. I thought about Phil, living alone on a piece of property that very soon would just keep booming and booming.

There is exactly one place at Walt Disney World where that boom ceased to be heard, and that is the Walt Disney World Preview Center. I pulled in and parked my car in the parking lot, hardly changed since 1970. I had been here before, of course. But today was different. Today I was going to go inside.

I had been to historic Disney locations before. But this one simply feels different than most. Marceline, Missouri, has had to re-create its Disney history, featuring as it does "Walt's Barn" (rebuilt in 2001) and "Walt's Dreaming Tree" (replanted in 2019). A lot of Disney history is like this, like the history he presented on Main Street USA—idealized, sentimentalized, basically faked. The Walt Disney World Preview Center isn't like that. You have to peer really hard to see the special that's hidden there. As you may have guessed by reading this book, that's the kind of history I love.

I ascended the steps and buzzed in on the intercom, and the door opened.

Since 1971, the Preview Center has been home to a rotating cast of tenants. Disney used it as a sales office for Lake Buena Vista starting in 1972 and even a furniture showroom under the direction of Emile Kuri. For a

July 2023, photo by the author.

while, it was a post office and a check-in lobby for the Lake Buena Vista Villas. But the Villas were set to become the Disney Institute in 1996, and the future of the Preview Center was in doubt.

Following the ugly debut of Disneyland Paris, Michael Eisner increasingly tuned out from the creative aspect of Disney's theme parks. He returned to his original creative muse, television—specifically acquiring television networks and sports teams.[194]

Eisner's creed was, anything he liked had to be represented at Walt Disney World—which is how the resort ended up with a dozen convention centers. To Eisner's credit, he didn't try to put in a professional sports stadium; Walt Disney World required a different kind of athletic complex. Instead, he lured the Atlanta Braves to Florida for spring training and reached out to the Amateur Athletic Union. After some negotiations, the AAU relocated from Indianapolis into the vacated Preview Center, where Disney wasn't even charging rent.[195] Since 1997, the AAU has continued its nationwide activities from this historic location as well as helped keep a steady stream of athletic events flowing through the Disney Wide World of Sports Complex down the road.

The move very likely saved the Preview Center from demolition.

Upon entering, what surprised me immediately was how massive the building was. From the outside, it's easy to write the Preview Center off as tiny, even underwhelming. Disney added a mansard roof and deep overhang around the exterior of the building, which disguises its true size, a theme park trick deployed where you least expect it. The interior, of course, is entirely changed. The original building's most noteworthy feature, those wide, sun-splashed galleries around its perimeter, have been filled in with offices. But very little was recognizable. I had come armed with a fleet of photos I wanted to try to match up but rarely felt compelled to open my bag.

But the center of the building, where the theater was, is still there. Standing in that room, it really hit me how I was standing in the 1960s-style attraction building, a space I knew well from working in the theme parks twenty years ago. From the concrete floor, I could look up to the steel girder ceiling installed by U.S. Steel fifty summers ago, and it reminded me of being behind the sets at Haunted Mansion or Hall of Presidents. It felt the same.

It put me a little in the mindset of how impressive a showplace this would have been in 1970. With its original fit and finish, wide hallways and orange juice bar, this building astonished Orlando locals. It's easy to look back at the actions of people in the past and write them off as hysterical or strange. But standing in that empty room, I began to understand why newspapers from Tallahassee to Miami encouraged Floridians to make the drive out and see Disney's Preview Center.

After fifteen minutes of wandering about poking my head into offices and break rooms, I thanked my tour guide, Kelsey, and left. From 1970 until 1971, 1.3 million visitors passed through that building. In the fifty years since then, I'd be surprised if I was among 50,000 who have seen its interior.[196]

I left Disney property onto State Road 535. Disney's strip mall, The Crossroads, had been torn down a few months before. The little spit of land bought by W.S. Stuckey alongside Interstate 4 is still there; today it's the location of a chain hotel and a Waffle House. The Stuckey's was moved to SR-192 in the 1980s and is now a thrift store. Mr. Clements, the savant of 535 who inspired Disney to build its own preview center, spent his life savings and bought a tiny piece of land across the street. That piece of land is now a gas station, and Mr. Clements probably died rich.[197]

I turned left onto 535 and drove past the gas station where Johnny's Corner used to be. Lost tourists seem to crawl around this intersection day and night. Jock Lowery's little house is now the site of a strip mall and Chinese restaurant. Fern Lowery, wife of Jock, lived to be ninety-six and continued

Above and opposite: July 2023, photos by the author.

living in a tiny house in Vineland until her death in 2010. I wondered what she and Phil Smith would think of the bustle of Vineland today.

When you live in Orlando—as I did for almost twenty years—your relationship with Walt Disney World changes. At first it's all Epcot and Dole Whips and rides on Tower of Terror. But after a while, you get tired of the parks. The heat starts to get to you, and the hassle of driving I-4, parking and walking in starts to become more and more noticeable.

Then you begin to notice that your friends start using your apartment as a free hotel, and you can't seem to get them interested in going to the great Korean place you know or driving to check out the new brewery in town. In 2019, 75.8 million people visited Orlando,[198] nearly 70 million of them

Courtesy of the Lake Buena Vista Historical Society.

from the United States. When these people tell you they've been to Orlando you can see in their eyes that they're thinking about the WonderWorks on International Drive or the giant Wizard gift shop on 192. They know nothing of the shaded cobblestone neighborhoods south of downtown, of the shops in Audubon Park—nothing of the diverse, tolerant and beautiful community you live in. Soon, you start to resent Disney just a little.

As a result, Central Floridians tend to treat Disney World as something different than Orlando, and the entire area south of Millenia starts to feel like a quarantine zone. Thousands of books have been published on Orlando history that hardly mention Disney at all, as if it is a known phenomenon—as if you can visit there and know everything there is to the place just on sight.

I hope this book changes that a little. Once you know how to look past the Disney history—the Main Streets and Chinese Theaters and Animal Kingdom Lodges—you can discover the Vinelands, the Carl Langfords, the Florida Centers, the Lake Buena Vistas that made all of that possible. Disney may have *made* Orlando, *but Orlando also made Disney*. It's real history, and it's waiting there for us to reclaim it.

Acknowledgements

Roy Disney and Disney leadership at Bay Lake. *Florida State Archives.*

This book would not have been possible without the support of the rest of the Disney history community over the course of the last two decades. Thanks to Mike Lee for leading the way, Michael and Jeff Crawford for being my fellow Disney History gremlins, Todd and the crew at Retro Disney World, Martin Smith and Brice and Brandon for being my sounding boards.

Significant help came from Stephanie Stuckey for trying to help me find Mr. Clements, Yesterworld Entertainment and Kevin Perjurer for filling in some gaps, the staff of the Orlando Public Library for tolerating me for the past twenty years, The DIX Index and Ted at DisneyDocs.Com for help locating rare documents. I received help from The Wolfson Archive at Miami-Dade College; The Dr. Phillips Foundation, which tolerated a lunatic asking about an old packinghouse; The Sarnoff Collection at College of

New Jersey for help on RCA and Disney for a deleted chapter; the *Orlando Sentinel* for some photographs; the *West Orange Observer* for a few articles; and the Saratoga Springs History Museum for introducing me to its ghost.

Thanks also to Tom Morris for his recollections, as well as Dave Ensign and How Bowers for sticking it out through the long haul. And a quiet remembrance of Jim Korkis, who was always kind to me when we talked.

NOTES

Prelude

1. Pierce, "Walt Disney and Riverfront Square."
2. Dunlop, *Building a Dream*, 117.

Part I. Miles of Worthless Land

3. *Orlando Sentinel*, October 1, 1971.
4. Jean, "Flashback."
5. Not a month goes by that I don't think about this nonsense.
6. "Orlando's Radio Nick," *Orlando Sentinel*, May 29, 1994.
7. Hawthorne, "Pre-Disney History of Discovery Island."
8. Anybody who knows the area well will justifiably have raised eyebrows at this, as even Vineland wasn't fully paved in those days—with 1940s automobile suspension, it must have been a long, slow drive over dirt roads.
9. August 30, 1945. I'm fairly certain that the dock was on the north end of Bay Lake. Aerials from 1952 show no development or roads on the south side, where Fort Wilderness is now, and that siren would be eccentric if the sound didn't have to travel the half mile across the lake. Okay, it's eccentric either way.
10. *Orlando Sentinel*, October 11, 1971.
11. *Orlando Sentinel*, September 28, 1981.
12. "Phil and Gwen in Disney World," *Orlando Evening Star*, June 24, 1967.
13. "Bob Welbaum: Four More Disney Legends Named by NFFC," Laughing Place, https://www.laughingplace.com.
14. Vagnini, "King of the World."
15. *Orlando Sentinel*, February 17, 1970.
16. Koenig, *Realityland*, 54.

17. Moryc, "Preview of Disney's Word," 44.
18. Disney renamed this lake Lake Buena Vista.
19. Disney used this information to know where to target advertising efforts on the opening of Walt Disney World, which is both logical and devious.
20. The gazebo is long gone, but the elevated "ridge" walkway leading to it from the Preview Center building remains very much in evidence.
21. *Fort Lauderdale News*, May 8, 1971.
22. Moryc, "Preview of Disney's Word," 48.
23. This is a private office complex; please don't try to go inside!
24. This point is contentious. The Phillips family was secretive in their affairs, and nobody has ever been able to figure out where "Doc" earned his medical degree. Following his death in 1959, I found a few people who claimed he practiced medicine as a young man in Ohio, except the good doctor was from Tennessee, so that can't have been him. My personal opinion is that Dr. Phillip Phillips was not a medical doctor, but the Phillips Foundation insists otherwise, so what do I know?
25. I'd love to know what this "special gift" was, although I suspect it was just an orange. Free orange!!!
26. Porte rand Evotek, *Historic Orange County*, 30.
27. Confirmed by the Dr. P. Phillips Foundation in private correspondence.
28. Korkis, *Unofficial Walt Disney World 1971 Companion*, 128.
29. Miller, *What Would Walt Do*, 82.
30. I suspect, but cannot prove, that certain items may have been sent to Florida via freight train. If this is the case, then the Phillips plant would have been the nearest location to receive these items before trucking them over to Magic Kingdom. But the official record here is inconclusive and so this "fact" must remain as a footnote.
31. Leaphart, *Walt Disney World Railroads*, 104.
32. The last documented reference to the packinghouse I can find is its lot being used as a school bus turnaround in 1977. No word on whether the old relic was still standing.

Part II. Action Center

33. Clark, *Orlando, Florida*, 68.
34. I'd love to know what room she stayed in—talk about an obscure but significant historical location.
35. "Walt Fenced, but Emily Bavar Knew," *Orlando Sentinel*, October 1, 1971.
36. Vagnini, "King of the World."
37. Korkis, *Unofficial Walt Disney World 1971 Companion*, 267.
38. Nunis, *Walt's Apprentice*, 171.
39. Snow, *Disney's Land*, 125.
40. Hill, "Texan with Big Dreams."
41. Korkis, "Lost Joe Potter Interview."
42. Korkis, *Unofficial Walt Disney World 1971 Companion*, 124.
43. Koenig, *Realityland*, 63.

44. Korkis, *Secret Stories*, 153.

45. *Orlandoland Magazine*, September 1971.

46. Koenig, *Realityland*, 73.

47. Korkis, *Unofficial Walt Disney World 1971 Companion*, 139.

48. *United States Steel Corporation 1969 Annual Report*, 20.

49. "Disney World: A Building Revolution," *Fort Lauderdale News*, May 10, 1969.

50. Koenig, *Realityland*, 69.

51. You may have heard that the rooms could be removed for future renovation, but this isn't true; the construction was a one-way trip.

52. Thomas, *Building a Company*, 320.

53. *Orlando Sentinel*, September 23, 1976.

54. Orange County Comptroller Document #19750916118.

55. *Orlando Sentinel*, November 22, 1970.

56. For those of you wondering, yes, Bob Morgan is a relative of Orlando icon John Morgan.

57. Today known as the Orlando Executive Airport.

58. *Miami Herald*, September 20, 1970.

59. *Tampa Tribune*, July 29, 1970.

60. This is still a thing; in 2019, Orlando International Airport sued Melbourne for calling itself the "Orlando Melbourne International Airport." This is only a little more deceptive than Sanford, which used to call itself the "Orlando Gateway International Airport." Sanford's airport is fifty miles away from Disney World; Melbourne's is seventy-five.

61. *Orlando Evening Star*, October 23, 1971; Carl Langford was Orlando's longest-serving mayor until the arrival of Buddy Dyer and was known for his bizarre hijinks; once, he stole the presidential seal off the White House podium by slipping it inside his jacket. His final act as mayor of Orlando was to play taps on a bugle inside city hall.

62. *Miami Herald*, December 30, 1972.

63. The idea of laying grooves in roads to play music is actually not unique to Disney World. A Honda dealership installed one of these stunts in Lancaster, California, in 2008, and National Geographic built another one on Route 66 through New Mexico in 2014. And if you look up any information about either of those attempts, you'll see that actually both of those promotional stunts were kind of failures: the one in California sounds terrible, and the one in New Mexico has been partially removed.

64. Diversified Food Systems was founded to bring Hardee's restaurants from North Carolina to Central Florida. Hardee's franchisors built a hotel.

65. This restaurant featured flambé dishes and Caesar salad tossed tableside and was famous in its early days for The Puzzle, an Orlando performing sextet whose motto was: "No cross words." I swear to God I'm not making this up. In later days, Limey Jim's would also host Weird WDW favs Saltwater Express.

66. Sadly, I've been unable to verify this astonishing story, but it was printed in the *Orlando Sentinel*, April 11, 1976, page 69, "Resolve Pays Off at Hyatt"—and some stories simply cannot go unrepeated.

67. *Orlando Sentinel*, August 7, 1969.
68. *Orlando Sentinel*, December 1, 1971.
69. If you are new to Orlando and hear somebody referring to the area where I-4 and Florida's Turnpike cross as "Florida Center," this is what they are referring to. This obsolete term is slowly dying out as more and more new residents move in, however.
70. Snow, *Disney's Land*, 314.
71. "Television Boosts Mattel," *Los Angeles Times*, December 20, 1970. Mattel was an early beneficiary of *The Mickey Mouse Club*, sponsoring a quarter hour of the initial run of the program for an eye-watering $500,000—an unheard-of sum in 1955. The company made it back many times over in Mickey Mouse Club toys, launched Barbie in 1959 and by the early '70s was a real rival for the Disney throne.
72. *Orlando Sentinel*, May 15, 1914.
73. Andrews, "Vineland."
74. Porter and Evotek, *Historic Orange County*, 83.
75. While researching the Phillips packinghouse in chapter 4, I was stymied by one errant historical detail. I was able to get the record to sync up for everything around the packinghouse that indicated it was demolished in 1977–78, except for one *Sentinel* article from December 1995 that claimed that it had burned down the previous night. I believe that the structure that burned was this sawmill, which everyone must have confused with the more famous Phillips packinghouse in the decades following its demolition. Such are the dangers of writing a book about a city where everyone is a recent transplant.
76. "Family's Store Helped Those in Need," *Orlando Sentinel*, April 23, 2010.

Part III. The Vacation Kingdom of the World

77. Nunis, *Walt's Apprentice*, 40.
78. Snow, *Disney's Land*, 323.
79. Surrell, *Pirates of the Caribbean*, 53.
80. And yes, this is why Magic Kingdom is the only park at Walt Disney World with a whole lot of rides.
81. Yes, there was *always* a fee for parking, even at Disneyland in the 1950s.
82. Surprisingly, Disney still honors this old policy. When I worked at Magic Kingdom in the early 2000s, I heard a story that a guest had arrived at Guest Relations with several intact ticket books from the 1970s and wanted to trade them in for modern-day passes. Cast members tried to convince the man not to do it, but he was adamant. The woman who took the ticket books in the back room cried as she cut them up to void them. Those books were worth many times the value of a 2004 day pass to Epcot.
83. This was the Midget Autopia—a real thing.
84. The design of Magic Kingdom actually began with Cinderella Castle, which was extensively workshopped, modeled, even tested for effectiveness with every angle

of the sun. The 198-foot landmark they ended up with was massive compared to Disneyland's quaint Sleeping Beauty Castle, and the size of the castle dictated a new design approach to Main Street.

85. Dunlop, *Building a Dream*, 129.

86. *Orlando Sentinel*, May 2, 1968.

87. Really an orange button—arguably a disappointment.

88. This grove lasted about a year before being cleared away for the Caribbean Plaza expansion, but knowing it was there does help contextualize Clyde's remark about "New Year's Eve in the orange grove" in the attraction preshow.

89. How I wish footage of this existed somewhere. If only every Florida politician were required to be heckled by robotic toucans.

90. *Tampa Tribune*, August 10, 1975.

91. *Orlando Sentinel*, December 5, 1980.

92. This was to be copied pretty much directly from the version of the Tropical Serenade, which opened at Tokyo Disneyland in 1983.

93. "Agribriefs," *Tampa Tribune*, May 3, 1987.

94. *Orlando Sentinel*, July 30, 1987.

95. Gabler, *Walt Disney*, 573.

96. McDonald, "Now the Bankers Come."

97. The Forest Service is distinct from the National Park Service in that their mandate is not necessarily preservation; the Forest Service tries to decide what the best use of public land should be—whether that be conservation, recreation or even timber production.

98. That road was the crux of the whole issue here; because it existed, Mineral King was public land, but it was not preserved public land. This distinction is important and gets lost in most discussions of Mineral King.

99. Selmi, *Dawn at Mineral King*, 31.

100. "The Disney Plans for Mineral King," Disney Docs collection, accessed December 2022.

101. A very similar debate played out in Prince William County, Virginia, surrounding Disney's America in the 1990s.

102. Merritt and Doctor, *Marc Davis*, 436–37.

103. What's at Walt Disney World today owes far more to Roy Disney than Walt Disney, and it was Roy who insisted that the project bear his little brother's name—not Disney World, but *Walt Disney World*. The man does not get enough credit for his incredible courage.

104. Thomas, *Building a Company*, 300.

105. *Daily National Democrat* (Marysville, CA), June 22, 1860.

106. *The E Ticket* No. 33, pg. 40.

107. Daveland Frontierland Shooting Gallery Page, https://www.davelandweb.com.

108. "Playing Nintendo Laser Clay in the Early 1970s," *beforemario*, http://blog.beforemario.com.

109. Sheff, *Game Over*, 27.

110. Parish, *NES Works*, 45.

111. Trade catalogs from Stroblite Co. Inc., National Museum of American History, https://americanhistory.si.edu.

112. "Night Lighting…How It's Done," Museum of the City of San Francisco, http://sfmuseum.org.

113. Snow, *Disney's Land*, 65.

114. Iwerks and Kenworthy, *Hand Behind the Mouse*, 185.

115. "Motion Picture Exhibition Techniques," accessed through the DIX index.

116. Nilsen, *Projecting America*, location 930.

117. The Soviets had a replica of the Sputnik I on display; it went missing, and of course everyone pointed fingers at each other.

118. Nilsen, *Projecting America*, location 1077.

119. As far as I know, after this film ended its run at Disneyland in 1966, it has never been seen again; a VHS release in the '80s is of the later remake version.

120. Iwerks and Kenworthy, *Hand Behind the Mouse*, 199.

121. Expo '67 is largely ignored by Americans due to the location in Canada and the existence of the 1964 World's Fair, but this expo was arguably a much larger influence on Epcot. Look up a picture of the fair, and you'll instantly know what I mean.

122. The Disney studio bitterly complained to the State Department that they ended up plowing $100,000 of their own money into *The USA in Circlevision* to complete it; this assertion is debatable, but regardless Disney ended up owning the film outright, so they got a great deal.

123. The 1939 and 1964 New York World's Fairs were unofficial in the sense that they were not approved by the organizing body behind the fairs. This would be like if you and I decided to hold the Olympics next year and dared the Olympics committee to stop us. This is a very New York thing to do but an even more Robert Moses thing to do.

Part IV. EPCOT, E.P.C.O.T. and All the Other Epcots

124. Thomas, *Building a Company*, 302.

125. Not coincidentally, this coincided with a very noisy public debate in Los Angeles concerning mass transit solutions. For the additional context you didn't know you needed, see Peter Dibble's excellent documentary "How Los Angeles Rejected the Monorail," https://youtu.be/piF7adQyXCk.

126. Gabler, *Walt Disney*, 324.

127. This is fascinatingly similar to Bob Iger's desire to sell Disney to Apple, the General Electric of today.

128. Korkis, *Unofficial Walt Disney World 1971 Companion*, 54.

129. Thomas, *Building a Company*, 303.

130. Roosevelt Island was, amazingly, previously used to house criminals and those deemed insane; by the 1960s, it was being turned into a planned community.

131. Flower, *Prince of the Magic Kingdom*, 62.

132. See my article, "The Weird History of Ports O' Call Village," *Passports to Dreams Old & New*, http://passport2dreams.blogspot.com.

133. Stewart, *Disney War*, 63.

134. *Progress City Radio Hour*, Episode 36, 28:50, https://www.podbean.com/ew/pb-4unfx-11091a3.

135. The idea is the "wedge" could be expanded to match the budget of each participant. This was still very much reflected in the design of the final park, although subsequent expansions have obscured the idea that each nation would have equal frontage along the lagoon.

136. Walt Disney Productions Annual Report 1975, 8.

137. Prizer, "Haunted by a Painting," 56.

138. Grover, *Disney Touch*, 208.

139. Merritt and Doctor, *Marc Davis*, 677.

140. Crawford, "Epcot Origins."

141. Of reliable sources, Koenig in *Realityland* is the principal source on this (167), although DeCuir does credit himself as such on his IMDb mini-biography: https://www.imdb.com/name/nm0214039/bio.

142. Goff had left Disney and designed a few themed shopping centers after Disneyland, and he knew what would appeal to the pedestrian.

143. Koenig, *Realityland*, 178.

144. All of this was part of a confusing and ill-conceived marketing angle to insist that all of Walt Disney World was Walt's "city of the future" and that the new park was a showcase for it. Once opening day passed, and everyone sobered up; no more was heard of this.

145. This sinkhole is sometimes blamed on leading to the closure of the Horizons pavilion, but that's just an urban legend. The Magic Kingdom sinkhole resulted in It's A Small World being scooted south a few yards; the resulting narrow passage was dismissively known as "Irvine Alley."

146. Flower, *Prince of the Magic Kingdom*, 84.

147. "A Chat with Claude Coats," Cartoon Research, https://cartoonresearch.com.

148. Kodak's chief rival was Fujifilm, which couldn't have helped.

149. Claude performed this same trick for Pirates of the Caribbean at Disneyland in 1963.

Part V. The Incredible Expanding Mouse

150. Thomas, *Building a Company*, 328.

151. Grover, *Disney Touch*, 12.

152. Flower, *Prince of the Magic Kingdom*, 91.

153. Grover, *Disney Touch*, 17.

154. Nunis, *Walt's Apprentice*, 146.

155. There is a special kind of weird Disney movie that Miller was spearheading in the late '70s and early '80s, a kind of panicked, urine-soaked hangover to the Lucas and Spielberg blockbusters that were changing the industry. The most famous of these is *TRON*, but also don't forget *Something Wicked This Way Comes*, *The Devil and Max Devlin* and *Watcher in the Woods*. These movies are fascinating

and kind of terrible, but you'll never forget them. *The Black Cauldron* may have been the capstone of all of this had it been released as intended, complete with decapitations and gory disintegrations.

156. The way this history repeated itself in 2022 with Bob Chapek and the modern successor to cable, streaming services, is truly fascinating.

157. Hale also was the creator of the Fire Fighters exhibit at the St. Louis World's Fair in 1904; buildings that appear to burst into flames for the approval of spectators remain a staple of the amusement industry even twelve decades later.

158. Fielding, "Hale's Tours."

159. Harmetz, "Man Re-Animating Disney."

160. Grover, *Disney Touch*, 66.

161. Disneyland favorites Billy Hill and the Hillbillies were actually hired to preside over these pig races; watch the whole show here: https://youtu.be/ylH5DxibEFk.

162. 20th Century Fox's Tom Sherack commented: "We'll lock the door and won't let him out until we have a deal."

163. Cosford, "Tinsel Town."

164. Eisner contributed substantially to the race.

165. Grover, *Disney Touch*, 176.

166. *Splash Too* is terrible, but it's amusing viewing for Walt Disney World fans. Locations used include Discovery Island, The Living Seas—posing as "Long Island Living Seas"—and at one point Amy Yasbeck has to say, "I went to the aquarium today to talk to Salty the Dolphin."

167. Only Michael Eisner would build an entire city street for a Bette Midler movie.

168. The sheer volume of newspaper ink wasted on *Superboy* in Central Florida newspapers between 1988 and 1990 really shows just how successfully Eisner and Graham sold the public on this notion.

169. Gennaway, *JayBangs*, 131.

170. If the proof is in the pudding, we need look no further than *Splash Too* and *Superboy* to see the limitations of the Florida studio. Both of those productions used Eisner's much-vaunted "Disney World is a backlot" strategy and look exactly like they were shot at, well, Disney World. Disney World may have diverse scenery, but its cartoonishly exaggerated colors are instantly identifiable.

171. Hinman, "Disney's New 'Baby.'"

172. If Orlando had a dime each time that happened, they would have two dimes!

173. Barry Diller is a fascinating sidebar to the Michael Eisner at Disney story, both a supporter and fly in the ointment. Diller and Eisner were considered a dream team that created such successes for Paramount as *Saturday Night Fever*, *Grease* and *Airplane!*. When Paramount was being split up, Diller went to News Corp, with Rupert Murdoch snapping up television stations around the country in a bid to create a new, fourth major television network. One of the big early successes for the Fox network was *DuckTales*, until Eisner pulled the show to a different station in Los Angeles. Diller responded by pulling the show off all of the Fox affiliate stations nationwide and starting up his own block of children's programming, Fox

Kids. The success of Fox Kids was instrumental in the growth of the Murdoch programming empire. So yes, a fight between these two men over *DuckTales* gave us *The Disney Afternoon, The Simpsons, Animaniacs, Mighty Morphin' Power Rangers, Batman: The Animated Series* and, yes, Fox News. The mind boggles.

174. Gennaway, *JayBangs*, 88.

175. The telling detail here is the trams. Trams were necessary at Universal Hollywood to transport guests up and down the hills that were part of Universal's property. Disney's Studio was built spec to be an attraction and was flat as a table—why include trams at all?

176. "Behind the MCA-Disney Tour War in Florida," *Los Angeles Times*, April 23, 1989.

177. Grover, *Disney Touch*, 74.

178. Ibid., 75.

179. This whole Tishman debacle really shows how bizarrely out of touch Card Walker was on this whole hotel thing. Tishman only got involved because Disney promised them that they could build and operate hotels at Disney World, just as they had with U.S. Steel. Walker's insistence on keeping Disney out of the hotel game may be the most confusing thing about a very confusing man.

180. Dunlop, *Building a Dream*, 63.

181. Gennaway, *Universal vs. Disney*, 91.

182 Dunlop, *Building a Dream*, 65.

183. I'd say that Dan Marino is the nearest degree of separation between Walt Disney World and *Ace Ventura: Pet Detective*...except that isn't true at all. There was actually an Ace Ventura stunt show and meet and greet at the Disney-MGM Studios on the Streets of America—where else?—probably the most cursed area of Walt Disney World.

184. Eisner's use of the term *Chautauqua* here is incredibly canny but also kind of meaningless. The Chautauqua movement of the nineteenth century was rooted in the politics of uplift and reform of the Industrial Revolution and most often took the form of a weeklong "educational vacation," often to some remote rural place.

185. For whatever reason, a lot of the promotion for the Disney Institute focused on that rock climbing wall, as if Disney World were missing that *one* vital component and would become a mecca for rock climbing enthusiasts.

186. Harmetz, "Man Re-Animating Disney."

187. Eisner, *Work in Progress*, 402.

188. *Orlando Sentinel*, April 30, 1991.

189. This author is fairly certain the attraction was being planned for the large empty parcels where World Drive passes below I-4 on the barren western side of town; there would otherwise seem to be very little point in connecting the new city to Walt Disney World's main tourist artery.

190. Grover, *Disney Touch*, 139

191. Pizza Hut got *Beauty and the Beast*.

192. "McDisney Production," *News Tribune*, May 24, 1996.

193. Nunis, *Walt's Apprentice*, 197.

Postscript

194. It's telling that his chosen successor came not from the movie studio or parks division but from ABC: Robert Iger.

195. "AAU Approves Move to Disney," *Orlando Sentinel*, September 10, 1994.

196. This location is in private offices, and I was on a tour as a researcher; please don't go trying to buzz yourself in!

197. This detail is remembered by D.M. Miller, who was there.

198. Orlando/Orange County Convention & Visitors Bureau 2019 Report.

BIBLIOGRAPHY

Andrews, Mark. "Vineland, A Community Time (Almost) Forgot." *Orlando Sentinel*, July 5, 1992.

Barrier, J. Michael. *The Animated Man: A Life of Walt Disney*. Berkeley: University of California Press, 2007.

Beard, Richard. *Walt Disney's EPCOT Center: Creating the New World of Tomorrow*. New York: Harry N. Abrams, 1982.

Bossert, David A. *Claude Coats: Walt Disney's Imagineer*. Los Angeles: Old Mill Press, 2021.

Bright, Randy. *Disneyland Inside Story*. New York: Harry N. Abrams, 1987.

Clark, James C. *Orlando, Florida: A Brief History*. Charleston, SC: The History Press, 2013.

Coats, Claude. Interview by Dan McLaughlin. Cartoon Research. https://cartoonresearch.com.

Cosford, Bill. "Tinsel Town of the Tropics." *Miami Herald*, July 4, 1982.

Crawford, Michael. "Epcot Origins: Becoming EPCOT Center." D23. October 2, 2012. https://d23.com.

———. *The Progress City Primer*. Orlando, FL: Progress City Press, 2013.

DeVore, Robert. "Phil and Gwen in Disney World." *Orlando Evening Star*, June 24, 1967.

"Doc Phillips and the Family." *Florida Magazine*, October 25, 1987.

Dunlop, Beth. *Building a Dream: The Art of Disney Architecture*. New York: Harry N. Abrams, 1996.

Eisner, Michael. *Work in Progress*. New York: Random House, 1998.

The "E" Ticket Magazine. Issue 30, Fall 1998.

———. Issue 33, Spring 2000.

Farley, Ellen. "Behind the MCA-Disney Tour War in Florida." *Los Angeles Times*, April 23, 1989.

Fielding, Raymond. "Hale's Tours: Ultrarealism in the Pre-1910 Motion Picture." *Cinema Journal*, Autumn 1970.

Fjellman, Stephen M. *Vinyl Leaves: Walt Disney World and America*. Boulder, CO: Westview Press, 1992.

Flower, Joe. *Prince of the Magic Kingdom: Michael Eisner and the Re-Making of Disney*. Hoboken, NJ: Wiley, 1991.

Fogelsong, Richard F. *Married to the Mouse: Walt Disney World and Orlando*. New Haven, CT: Yale University Press, 2003.

Gabler, Neal. *Walt Disney: The Triumph of the American Imagination*. New York: Vintage Books, 2007.

Gennaway, Sam. *JayBangs: How Jay Stein, MCA, & Universal Invented the Modern Theme Park and Beat Disney at Its Own Game*. Orlando, FL: Theme Park Press, 2016.

———. *Universal vs. Disney: The Unofficial Guide to American Theme Parks' Greatest Rivalry*. Birmingham, AL: Keen Communications, 2015.

Gordon, Bruce, and David Mumford. *Disneyland: The Nickel Tour*. Los Angeles: Camphor Tree, 2000.

Grover, Ron. *The Disney Touch*. Burr Ridge, IL: Business One Irwin, 1991.

Haden-Guest, Anthony. *The Paradise Program*. New York: William Morrow & Company, 1973.

Harmetz, Aljean. "The Man Re-Animating Disney." *New York Times Magazine*, December 29, 1985.

Hass, Charlie. "Disneyland Is Good for You." *New West Magazine*, December 4, 1978.

Hawthorne, Ginger. "The Pre-Disney History of Discovery Island." *RetroWDW*, August 14, 2019. https://www.retrowdw.com.

Hill, Barry R. *Imagineering an American Dreamscape: Genesis, Evolution, and Redemption of the Regional Theme Park*. N.p.: Rivershore Press, 2020.

Hill, Jim. "Texan with Big Dreams + Big Apple = Big Trouble." New York's World Fair. http://nywf64.com.

Hinman, Catherine. "Disney's New 'Baby' Drops By." *Orland Sentinel*, October 8, 1991.

History of Disney Theme Parks in Documents. https://www.disneydocs.net.

Iwerks, Leslie, and John Kenworthy. *The Hand Behind the Mouse*. New York: Disney Editions, 2001.

Jakle, John A. *City Lights: Illuminating the American Night*. Baltimore: Johns Hopkins University Press, 2001.

Jean, Charlie. "Flashback: Central Florida's Greatest Mystery." *Orlando Sentinel*, September 28, 1981.

Jones, Robert A. "How Disney Resort Plans Went Awry." *Los Angeles Times*, March 22, 1978.

Kern, Kevin, Tim O'Day and Steven Vagnini. *A Portrait of Walt Disney World*. New York: Disney Editions, 2021.

Koenig, David. *Mouse Tales*. Irvine, CA: Bonaventure Press, 1994.

———. *Realityland*. Irvine, CA: Bonaventure Press, 2004.

Korkis, Jim. "The Lost Joe Potter Interview." Mouse Planet. August 13, 2014. https://www.mouseplanet.com.

———. *Secret Stories of Walt Disney World*. N.p.: Theme Park Press, 2015.

———. *The Unofficial Walt Disney World 1971 Companion*. N.p.: Theme Park Press, 2019.

Kurtti, Jeff. *Since the World Began*. New York: Disney Editions, 1996.

———. *Walt Disney's Imagineering Legends*. New York: Disney Editions, 2008.

Langford, David L. "Johnny's Braces for Boom." *Orlando Sentinel*, November 22, 1970.

Leaphart, David. *Walt Disney World Railroads, Part 3: Yucatan Jewels*. Self-published, CreateSpace, 2016.

Lightman, Herb A. "Circling Italy with Circarama." *American Cinematogapher*, March 1962.

Marling, Karal Ann. *Designing Disney's Theme Parks: The Architecture of Reassurance*. New York: Flammarion, 1998.

Masters, Kim. *Keys to the Kingdom: How Michael Eisner Lost His Grip*. New York: William Morrow, 2000.

McDonald, John. "Now the Bankers Come to Disney." *Fortune Magazine*, May 1966.

Merritt, Christopher, and Pete Doctor. *Marc Davis in His Own Words*. New York: Disney Editions, 2020.

Miller, D.M. *What Would Walt Do?* Self-published, iUniverse, 2001.

Moryc, Matt. "A Preview of Disney's World." *2020 Hyperion Historical Alliance Annual*, 2020.

"Motion Picture Exhibition Techniques at Disneyland." *Business Screen Magazine*, September 1955.

Nilsen, Sarah. *Projecting America, 1958*. Jefferson, NC: McFarland, 2011.

Nunis, Dick. *Walt's Apprentice*. New York: Disney Editions, 2022.

Parish, Jeremy. *NES Works 1985*. Press Run, 2015.

Pierce, Todd James. *Three Years in Wonderland*. Jackson: University of Mississippi Press, 2016.

———. "Walt Disney and Riverfront Square Part 6." Disney History Institute. https://www.disneyhistoryinstitute.com.

Porter, Tania Mosier, and Cassandra Evotek. *Historic Orange County: The Story of Orlando and Orange County*. San Antonio, TX: HPN Books, 2009.

Prizer, Edward L. "Disney Count Down." *Orlandoland Magazine*, September 1971.

———. "Haunted by a Painting." *Orlando Magazine*, October 1982.

———. "Last Train to EPCOT Center." *Orlando Magazine*, October 1982.

Ridgway, Charlie. *Spinning Disney's World*. Branford, CT: Intrepid Traveler, 2007.

Selmi, Daniel P. *Dawn at Mineral King Valley*. Chicago: University of Chicago Press, 2022.

Sheff, David. *Game Over*. New York: Knopf Doubleday, 1994.

60 Minutes. "Will Mickey Mouse Eat Up Orange County?" CBS, June 18, 1972.

Sklar, Marty. *Dream It! Do It! My Half-Century Creating Disney's Magic Kingdoms*. New York: Disney Editions, 2013.

———. *Travels with Figment*. New York: Disney Editions, 2019.

Snow, Richard. *Disney's Land*. New York: Scribner, 2019.

Stewart, James R. *Disney War*. New York: Simon & Schuster, 2005.

Surrell, Jason. *The Disney Mountains: Imagineering at Its Peak*. New York: Disney Editions, 2007.

———. *Pirates of the Caribbean: From the Magic Kingdom to the Movies*. New York: Disney Editions, 2005.

Thomas, Bob. *Building a Company*. New York: Disney Editions, 1998.

———. *Walt Disney: An American Original*. New York: Disney Editions, 1994.

United States Steel Corporation 1969 Annual Report. Report No. 68. USS, 1969. Digital collection, Case Western Reserve University.

United States Steel Corporation 1970 Annual Report. Report No. 69. USS, 1970. Digital collection, Case Western Reserve University.

United States Steel Corporation 1971 Annual Report. Report No. 70. USS, 1971. Digital collection, Case Western Reserve University.

Vagnini, Steven. "King of the World: What It Was Like to Live at Walt Disney World." D23. https://d23.com.

Walt Disney Imagineering: A Behind the Dreams Look at Making the Magic Real. New York: Disney Editions, 1996.

Walt Disney Imagineering: A Behind the Dreams Look at Making More Magic Real. New York: Disney Editions, 2010.

Walt Disney Productions Annual Report. Disney, 1964–1983.

Walt Disney World: The First Decade. Walt Disney Productions Souvenir Book, 1981.

Whicker's World. "Pixie Dust on Goody-Goody Land." ITV TV, July 19, 1971.

Younger, David. *Theme Park Design & The Art of Themed Entertainment.* N.p.: Inklingwood Press, 2016.

Zehnder, Leonard E. *Florida's Disney World: Promises and Problems.* Tallahassee, FL: Peninsular Publishing Company, 1975.

Also by Foxx Nolte

Boundless Realm: Deep Explorations Inside Disney's Haunted Mansion

Scoundrels, Villains & Knaves: Disneyland, Pirates of the Caribbean, and Popular Culture

Visit us at
www.historypress.com
···